THE SATANIC NURSES

Also by J.B. Miller

My Life in Action Painting

THE SATANIC NURSES

And Other Literary

Parodies

J.B. Miller

Thomas Dunne Books   New York
St. Martin's Press

This book is a collection of parodies of many of the acclaimed writers of our day. Don't believe a word of it.

THOMAS DUNNE BOOKS.
An imprint of St. Martin's Press.

www.stmartins.com

Design by Phil Mazzone

Library of Congress Cataloging-in-Publication Data

Miller, J.B.
     The satanic nurses : and other literary parodies / J.B. Miller.
         p. cm.
     "Thomas Dunne books."
     ISBN 0-312-30544-3
     1. Parodies.   I. Title.

 PN6231.P3 M55 2003
 813'.54—dc21

                                                     2002035319

First Edition: January 2003

10 9 8 7 6 5 4 3 2 1

CONTENTS

CONTENTS

ACKNOWLEDGMENTS

The author would like to thank various people and institutions without whom (and without which) this impertinent collection would not have been possible: Lori Perkins, Sally Kim, Jim Gialamas, the Housing Works Bookstore Café (and its many kind denizens and helpful books), Salon.com, and everyone in zip code 10012.

INTRODUCTION

Shortly before he joined the Central European Bowling League, Vladimir Nabokov called me up at my Woodstock hideaway. It was difficult to hear "Vlad" (as everyone called him) because I had Lillian Hellman★ and Mary McCarthy duking it out in the kitchen.

"Hey—girls! Will you keep it down!"

Finally there was quiet.

"Sorry, Vlad, what were you saying?"

"I was saying, could you proofread a short story of mine? I don't trust any of my editors to do it."

"Why not?" I asked.

"They sometimes find things."

Truer words were never spoken, and it goes some way to explaining my close and uncritical friendship with so many of the finest writers of this, and maybe one other, generation. While maintaining a low profile as a regular citizen, I have managed to befriend and mentor many of these great wordsmiths, and I am happy to present here some of their lesser-known work. They could be very demanding, these ink-stained wretches, but I treasure

---

★Full disclosure: I was briefly married to Hellman in the early 1960s.

my time with them and have always been happy to help them. They entrusted these pieces to me on the understanding that I would never share them with anyone. So here they are.

A couple of weeks after my phone conversation with Nabokov, a brown package arrived in the mail. Inside I found "Colita," evidently a variation on his famous novel *Lolita*. By the time I called him with some comments, his snippy wife, Vera, told me that Vlad had just gone bowling in Geneva. (Again? Every time I called it was either bowling, miniature golf, or mah-jongg. Whatever it was, it always prevented Vlad from coming to the phone.) Anyway, I include the story in this collection, as well as an early version of J. R. R. Tolkien's masterpiece, *The Lord of the Rings*—or rather, a hitherto unknown early crack at that famous trilogy, a collection of notes for something that was going to be called "The Lord of the Strings." It isn't very good, but it's in here. Tolkien used to make prank phone calls, very late at night, pretending to be a pizza delivery man from Bag End, and I finally had to change my number.

Another telephone pest was J. D. Salinger, who used to call me up at all hours, day or night, begging me to take a look at his vast Glass saga—a tome he claimed was over three thousand pages and "in dire need of some goddam pruning." Perhaps I should have taken him up on the offer, but I remember Jack Kerouac often asked me to do the same thing, and getting through his later work could be quite a chore. He used to phone from his mother's house in Florida, where he spent a lot of his time watching TV. If I recall correctly, he used to call me up whenever *The Galloping Gourmet* was on, insisting that I tune in. Usually I had better things to do, such as typing up Edward Albee's stage directions. Albee appreciated my speed and accuracy as a typist, and he used to drive over in his VW Thing and recite his latest character cues. (By the way, it was I who suggested the title for *Who's Afraid of Virginia Woolf?* He wanted to call it *Who's Afraid of Pearl S. Buck?*)

Speaking of Virginia Woolf, I was barely nine years old when the Bloomsbury Group adopted me (illegally, it later turned out) to run small errands and do sundry cooking and cleaning in their various houses (Lytton Strachey I remember as a particularly lascivious slob). Notoriously short on toilet paper, the Woolves usually kept a pile of correspondence by the loo in lieu of bathroom tissue. One morning even this had run out, and I was forced to run into the library for some paper. The only thing close at hand was a coarsely bound volume on the desk. I tore out a handful of pages and rushed back to the WC. Needing only half the paper, I shoved the other half into my pocket and subsequently transferred them to my tuck box. It was many years later that I found the pages and discovered them to be entries from Virginia's celebrated diary, and I've included an excerpt in this collection. (My sojourn with the Bloomsbury gang ended badly; I was fired after a weekend at Monks House, where I washed off all of Vanessa Bell's murals in the living room. It was an honest mistake; I'd thought they were a vandal's graffiti.)

After I moved to New York, I briefly lived at the Waldolf Astoria, where Cole Porter was a frequent guest. It was Cole who taught me how to bowl. He was an avid bowler, and we used to spend hours in the hotel basement, bowling and writing lyrics. Eventually it became a source of friction, as he never gave me credit for steering him to the right words in "Kiss Me, Kate." (Does "Brush Up Your Marlowe" make any sense? No, I didn't think so either.) Anyway, I'm including in this collection the lyrics he penned (and lost) for "You're Full of Crap." He could be a right bastard when he wanted to be, and he wanted to be quite often. After the terrible skiing accident that left him partially paralyzed, he became something of a recluse, and I didn't see him much after I moved to my three-room walkup in swinging Greenwich Village. The early sixties were then in full phlegm, and I often hung out at Folk City and the Bitter End, helping a young, nearly illiterate troubadour with his convoluted lyrics (to this day, Dylan never even sends me so much as a Hanukkah card).

And then there was Hemingway. The last time I saw Pappy (as we all called him), we were shotgun shopping in Ketchum, Idaho. As I was looking at the small firearms and weighing a Glock 9mm in my right hand, I looked around and couldn't help noticing him experimentally placing a Wesson double-barreled shotgun in his mouth. "Too small," he muttered to himself.

"Hey, Pap—we're going to the cigar shop *next,*" I said with a laugh. Hemmy stared at me frostily. Two weeks later he was dead— of a massive heart attack. It was a surprise to many—but not me; I'd been watching him gobble up the cheeseburgers for years.

Anyway, I got a job tending bar at that famous West Village writer's watering hole, the Red Lion. For many years Joyce Carol Oates★ also bartended there, usually writing books between serving drinks (her average output was three books a week, but that could slow to a trickle around St. Patrick's Day). Frequent visitors included Terry McMillan (usually guy hunting), John Irving (we built him a special stool so he could reach the bar), and Jay McInerney, who called everyone "sport" and used to try to cadge free drinks by claiming to be a the cocktails critic for *Consumer Reports.* I was there one night when he brought in a baby-faced preppie he introduced as a "the future poet laureate of the drugged-out, MTV Generation." It didn't seem like anything to boast about, but we humored Bret Easton Ellis, and he proceeded to tell a long, tedious story about various people sleeping with other various people at Bennington. I told him he'd probably be happier selling ties at Brooks Brothers, to which he got very indignant and called me "an American psycho." I like to think I inspired him.

Norman Mailer liked to box patrons in the men's room, until we gave him a job as a bouncer (which let him keep out adversaries like Gore Vidal and Audrey Hepburn).

Philip Roth sometimes came in to the Red Lion, but he usually insisted on sitting in front of a mirror, and we couldn't always accommodate him. One particularly noisy evening, I remember, he came in looking very down in the dumps and said he was suffering from some sort of "complaint." I said, "I know what you mean. You can really pick that up at a port—boy!"

"Portnoy?" he said, not understanding me.

"Sure, whatever." I didn't want to have to explain myself—the

★Full disclosure: I was briefly married to Oates in the early 1970s.

place was too busy. Imagine my surprise when I saw the title of his next book. In thanks, he's graciously contributed a horrific autobiographical episode to this collection.

Another complainer was Frank McCourt, who used to bore everyone silly with his sob stories of eating cat stew in Limerick. But Frank was a fine friend, and he was always there to borrow money or cadge a drink.

By the early eighties I felt it was time to get out of New York and I went out west to become a cowboy with Cormac McCarthy. Contrary to popular opinion, Cormac is not such a good horseman, and during our trip across Wyoming, he preferred to travel by sidecar, insisting that I drive the Kawasaki we'd stolen from out front of a Laundromat in Cody.

It was on that trip that I first met Raymond Carver—or "Carve" to his friends. Carve, Corm, and I spent many mornings smoking unfiltered Camels and drinking quarts of Mad Dog.

Carve hated the movies, and said he was glad he'd never sold the film rights to any of his stories (not that anyone was actually interested in them at the time).

Raymond Carver and P. G. Wodehouse are not names you would normally associate, but few writers were not more inseparable. Carve and P.G. (or "Pluck," to his friends) used to go drag racing together on the Nevada flats, and it was there they decided to open a divorce ranch, just outside Reno. It was poor timing, as the doors to "Rancho Anullo" opened at the beginning of the infamous "divorce drought" of 1966–72, and the enterprise quickly went bankrupt. (The only successful divorce they hosted was between Eva Gabor and David Hockney—but even that turned out to be a bust when it was discovered they'd never been married in the first place; they just liked to go on vacation together.) Pluck was forced to move to L.A., where he played the wacky English neighbor for two seasons on *The Jeffersons,* and Carve returned to Washington state where he became a driver for a young computer entrepreneur named Bill Gates. Unfortunately Carve neglected to invest in Gates's start-up, and he lived out the rest of his days ironically as an usher at the Springfield Mall Regency Movie Theater.

What can I say about Toni Morrison that hasn't already been said—except that she's a lousy cook? And I mean terrible—after the third time I'd gotten food poisoning from her supposedly "delectable" salmon lemon mousse, I begged off any future dinner invitations (I consider myself lucky to be alive), and suggested we meet at a restaurant. She agreed, and we had an agreeably uneventful meal at a local Denny's. As usual, she plied me for career advice. This is what I told her: "Keep doing what you're doing—but try to pick up the pace a bit." The verdict is still out on whether or not she's followed this advice. What I do know is that she didn't pick up the check. Story of my life.

Anaïs Nin★ was another parsimonious friend; she used to do all her underwear shopping at Marks & Spencer (well, who doesn't?). The summer we spent together on Crete was truly magical, and I look back on her with great affection—except for the time she got so upset at a negative review of *Delta of Venus* in *Le Cahiers du Cinema* that she beat up a waiter (and the poor guy wasn't even French).

Anne Rice gets violent too, and there are pictures of her with red lines through them on the walls of so many bars, I actually published a *Guide to Eating and Drinking Establishments Which Ban Anne Rice* (six weeks on the *New York Times* Bestseller List, though the film has been in "development hell" for years).

Eve Ensler† is a friend from way back, and a great boxing and wrestling enthusiast. She struggled with her writing career after her success with the *Vagina Monologues* (a great subject, suggested by yours truly after she'd announced she was working on "The Upper Thigh Monologues." I said, "Eve—if you're going to do it, you might as well go all the way."). Anyway, she was stumped for a follow-up, so I put her in touch with Anne Rice, with whom I'd just gone witch-wrangling in the bayou, and they came up with the very moving dramatic piece, *The Vampire Monologues,* in this collection.

It was Saul Bellow himself who forwarded the curious correspondence from that aging British *enfant terrible* Martin Amis. I actu-

---

★Full disclosure: I was briefly married to Nin in the late 1950s.
†Full disclosure: I was never married to Ensler.

ally know Martin (or "Amis," as his friends call him) from our days on the executive committee of the famous Gaucho Club in London. The Gaucho, on Frith Street in Soho, was founded by Argentinean cowboy émigrés in the early sixties, and over the years it has nabbed more than a few members away from the oppressive Harpo Club on Pall Mall, which has always forbidden its signatories to speak.

When William Burroughs was living in London, his incessant mumbling got him kicked out of the Harpo and he was forced to join the Zeppo, which must be the most boring club in England. Perhaps he livened things up a bit there. I tend to doubt it. In the few conversations I had with him at "the Zep," he kept going on about "the lost boys of the Interzone" and how peanut butter was a government plot (for what, he never explained).

I preferred "the Gauch," where the ancient great polar explorer Ernest Shackleton sometimes shuffled into the nonsmoking room, usually overdressed, and he always told the same story about how he made it across southwest London without losing a single man. To shut him up I finally had him write it all down, and to pad out the word length of my book I've included it in this collection.

I met Samuel Beckett at a Bah Mitzvah in Riverdale. He was drunk, of course, and made a sloppy pass at one of the caterers (coincidentally, a girl I knew from the Actor's Studio, who didn't know who Beckett was). I managed to get some coffee into him and drove him back to the city, as he babbled on about Tolkien and recited both parts of "En Attendant Frodo," included in this book. I liked Beckett, but could rarely deal with him on his pub crawls, and he had an embarrassing tendency to attack any woman in a uniform.

It was Martin Amis who introduced me to Don DeLillo, who for years has had postalphobia. When I encouraged him to "write through" his fears, he came up with the interesting (if rather De-Lilloesque) fragment, "American Opener."

I've known Elmore Leonard since the days we both worked as pin monkeys in the same bowling alley in Barstow, California, years before either one of us became famous. One day Governor Reagan came by, telling us about his war experiences on the Western Front, and asking us to tear down all the surrounding trees as they were an environmental hazard.* Everyone found him very funny, and we were highly amused when he was later elected president. I didn't keep in touch with him much over the years, but when word went out that I was putting together this compendium of literary pieces, I received his contribution in the mail, along with a check for $22.91 and the confession that he'd walked off with his rented bowling shoes all those years ago. But the amount still doesn't make sense to me.

Some years ago a British publisher asked me if I could translate David Mamet's prose works into English. I told him regretfully that I just didn't have the time, and suggested Irvine Welsh as the man for the job. Welsh is usually the man for the job, unless the job is looking after your cat. (Irv claims he was gone for only two days, but when I got back, Professor Whiskers looked like he'd been dead for weeks.)

Kurt Vonnegut was still a struggling young science fiction writer when I encouraged him to write a novel about his war experiences. "But nothing happened to me," he complained. "I was just a dumb fuck who was taken prisoner and sent to Dresden."

"Look into it," I told him. "There might be something there."

Tom Wolfe could never be said to have low self-esteem, so I'll say it: Tom Wolfe had low self-esteem. The man in the famous white suit used to worry about his ignorance of popular culture, which unfortunately was his principal subject. Another late-night caller, he'd phone me up at three in the morning. "J.B., I know *nothing* about anything. What am I *doing* in this business? I make everything up!"

"Calm down, Tom, you're fine. But if you're going to make everything up, why don't you become a novelist?"

Admittedly, this took several years to sink in, but he finally took

---

*Reagan claimed the trees were dangerously using up the local oxygen. I've been nervous around plant life ever since.

my advice and squeezed out a couple of fat novels. The white suit, unfortunately, I could do nothing about.

Fay Weldon has improved my catalogue reading no end, and I particularly appreciate the work she's done on Lands' End, Tweed, and Victoria's Secret. This collection includes her lesser-known work on the Hampton catalogue, "The Evil Pajamas."

E. Annie Proulx has always been a good sport about my joshing (except for the one time she went at me with a potato peeler). She's a fun gal, but never go camping with her. Trust me.

Nicholson Baker, the hyperrealist technician, once came over at a moment's notice to help me put together a step-ladder-clock-lamp that had indecipherable instructions. Unfortunately, all he did was rewrite the instructions and get them published by Grove/Atlantic, but it was still helpful.

That popular a cappella group the Footnotes (Dave Eggers, Rick Moody, David Foster Wallace, and Jonathan Franzen—until he was kicked out for insufficient sourcing) were for years a regular attraction at the Bitter End, and I used to hum along as best I could. The later dissonant stuff I found harder to get into, but they're a friendly bunch who've never meant anyone any harm.

John Updike, that Renaissance man with the big shelf—I salute thee. Rabbit, long thought dead, makes a return visit from the grave in the instructive narrative "Rabbit Rocks," which Updike somehow forgot to publish.

J. K. Rowling, the hot babe/billionaire, is the sweetest soul, and thank God she ignored my advice—i.e., "Better make it Hester Potter—everyone knows boys don't read books, and girls don't read books with boy protagonists. And with Hester, you'll have the Scarlet Letter/adultery theme to play with. Also, lose the witch/wizard thing. Too old hat. Why not a barber school? Or costume jewelry?" Her contribution to this anthology, "Harry Potter and the Rolling Stone," displays a hitherto unknown affinity for British Invasion rock. Will Harry ever need a complete blood transfusion in Zurich? Will Hermione join an ashram in Poona? Can Hogwarts realistically host a ten-day music and crafts festival with only twelve portable toilets? Stay tuned.

. . .

Shortly after the Fatwa was announced on Salman Rushdie, he showed up at my apartment in New York and asked if he could stay the night. I was understandably nervous about this, but he slept on the fold-out couch and ended up staying several months. Things began well enough; Sal spent most of his time inside, listening to my CDs and watching my videos. But after a while he wanted to go out, and insisted on wearing my clothes, so (as he said) he could "play" me and not be identified. Later, this "role-playing" extended to wearing my Versace silk suits and borrowing my credit cards, and after he racked up over three hundred dollars in late fees on my Kim's video account, I decided it was time to put my foot down. I encouraged him to move on. He did, finally, helping himself to my Velvet Underground box set, and we haven't spoken since. I don't know where he went. Wherever he is, I wish him well—though I wouldn't mind my Velvet CDs back.

And so I offer up these pieces, humbly (and quickly, before too many of the living authors reach for their attorneys), creating a portrait, of sorts, of the modern canon. I hope it doesn't blow me up.

If there is one universal among all these pieces, it's how different they all are. And yet, in some ways, they all could have been written by the same man. I like to think, as one of the finest friends to great authors everywhere (and with one of the more modest of personalities), that man could have been me.

—J.B. Miller
May 2002

ERNEST HEMINGWAY

HUNTING A TIGER IN AFRICA

This story, which I found behind a filing cabinet in a maintenance closet at Esquire magazine, is believed to be Hemingway's last unpublished work. It concerns an ill-fated safari the author took to the African Congo in November 1957, when he was thought to be in the middle of a five-day drunk at the Ritz Hotel in Paris. I have left the text exactly as Hemingway wrote it, except for occasional routine corrections of spelling, grammar, punctuation, structure, and narrative. I also changed the title from the author's original, less poetic "African Tiger Piece—Crap—Do Not Publish."

The mornings were thin and dry and the purple sky hung low off the green hills. We had been camping out on the plains for three weeks looking for the tiger and we had not yet found it, but the room service had been very good. Every morning we had eggs and bacon and ham and beans and brioche and Mary had Café au lait and I had pernod with pernod, and they were wonderful breakfasts. We'd lie in bed and make love in the morning and then have breakfast again and then listen to Miss Piaf on the radio. This morning was no different from the other mornings except that I had an extra pernod with pernod and Mary ate her brioche with a spoon instead of a fork and then she looked at me severely.

"You're not going hunting in *that,* are you?"

"I was planning to, yes."

I changed into my gray Brooks Brothers suit with the fine weave and my Oxford shoes. We looked for the tiger, the one with my name written on it. There were no tigers but there were elks and giraffes and gazelles and we shot all of them. If you want to kill an animal you have to respect it and then you have to love it and then you have to kill it. It is not easy to kill a thing you admire so much, but as the homosexual writer Oscar Wilde said, every man kills the thing he loves.

It was then on the plain in the middle of the tall grasses that I saw him standing, tall and majestic. It was an old lion but it had Mary's name on it. Why someone would write MARY on the side of a lion is anybody's guess, but there it was and there was nothing to do, Mary had to shoot it. I handed her the gun. She aimed and fired. She missed the lion with her name on it and shot the lion with my name on it. It was a bigger lion because my name is a bigger name, and it went down heavily.

"Sorry, Hem, I shot your lion."

"It doesn't matter."

"It does matter. I know you're upset."

"Forget it. It was just a lion."

"But didn't you want it?"

"No, it doesn't matter. Let's go back to the camp, I have to pee."

At the base camp I found the men's room. There was only one urinal, made entirely of ivory, and Scott Fitzgerald was standing at it, staring down at his genitals. "Hey, Hem," he said in his slightly girlish voice, which worried you, until you thought about it, and then it worried you even more. "Do you think my penis is too small?"

"It's fine, Scott. Zip up and go home to your wife."

"But doesn't it look small?" He squinted down at his equipment, and then he squinted some more. Then he stopped squinting.

"You're looking at it from a bad angle," I told him. "It's fine. Go home and make love to your wife. Put a pillow under her ass. Just get out of the way, I have to piss."

Fitzgerald got out of the way. I stepped up, unzipped, and started pissing. I thought of how the elks piss—always standing up and holding their penises tightly with their front hoofs. I thought of elephants pissing, lifting up a hind leg like a large dog. Then I thought of the lion with my name on it, how Mary had shot it and how it would never piss again.

We had lunch in a little place called Chez Mitzi, not far from Mount Kilimanjaro, around the corner from the Place Vendôme. I had a pernod with a whiskey and Mary had a Camembert milkshake, which she said was not so good. Afterward, coming out of the revolving doors, Mary caught one of her fingers on the edge of the door, and I said there was nothing to do in a case like this, we'd have to deal with it. It was a long way from the base camp and we'd never get a cab now, not with the rain like it was. We couldn't leave her there because then the wild game would get her or maybe the hat check girl. It was best to deal with it now, quickly and surely as things had to be done.

"It's only a bruise, Hem. Just give me a Band-Aid."

I knew she was being brave and the best thing would be to put her out of her misery and shoot her as we had done with poor little Bumby when he fell off his tricycle in Cuba. It was a tough thing to do, but not as tough as not doing it, and as with Bumby it had to be done. I took my Wesson double-barreled shotgun and shot Mary just behind the left ear. It was a clean shot and she went down heavily like the old lion with my name on it.

It is a Zulu custom that what you kill you have to eat. It is a good custom. I dragged Mary back to the base camp and we cooked her up with an Alfredo cream sauce. It tasted like chicken. The Zulu chief thanked me and gave me a teenage Wakamba love slave called Iris Grendale. She was black as the African night and she said she'd just finished her freshman year at Vassar and was working as an intern at *Glamour* magazine or maybe it was *Mademoiselle*. It didn't matter. She had high cheekbones and high breasts and an expense account. All she talked about was shopping at Saks Fifth Avenue and Bergdorf-Goodman and B. Altman and Bloomingdale's, and I told her I didn't much care for shopping and then I told her to shut up. We went into her tent. All over the walls were pictures of Mr. Presley and Mr. Brando. We made love, quickly and severely, and then I left to go out hunting again.

I walked several hours on the plains. The light was turning gray as the sun was going down over the green hills of Africa, and I saw a large, heavy animal peeing majestically with its hind hooves holding its proud penis. It was not an African tiger, it was a marshelt, which looks more like an African tiger than an African tiger does—if you don't know what an African tiger looks like. I let it go. I felt bad about having shot Mary after she shot my lion and eating her with the Zulu doctor, but it was the way of the jungle and it was what you had to do. And what else could you do anyway? And then there was Iris Glendale. And besides, there was a party in Tent 11B.

When I got back to the base camp Marlene Dietrich was standing at the billiard table and she was up nine hundred dollars. The Zulus were brave, majestic people, but they were not good billiard players. The Kraut looked over at me.

"It goes?"

"It goes."

"I heard what happened with Mary."

"It happened."

"Just as well. She was a lousy cook."

"Nevertheless."

"Yes, nevertheless."

The party was getting very crowded now and someone started a conga line. I stood by the side of the tent and watched the young people enjoy themselves the way young people do. The witch doctor, whom the local natives had taken to calling "Bully Willis" after he won the middleweight boxing championship in Chicago in 1926, asked me what I was doing in the Congo.

"Hunting a tiger," I told him.

"There are no tigers in Africa," said Bully.

I thought about this for a while, and then I thought some more, and then I stopped thinking.

"In that case, Bully, just give me a double Scotch."

"Right you are, Papa. Coming right up."

VLADIMIR NABOKOV

COLITA

Colita, cold comforter of my carefree existence, lifeless frame that she is. Co-lee-ta.

She was Co, sweet Co in the morning, washing her dentures in the sink. She was Cola in the backseat, sipping a soft drink. She was Nana Co to the strange crew of her California family, but to me, in my arms, she was always Colita.

Were there precursors? Indeed there were. In point of fact, had it not been for the old geezers I used to visit after school at the Rivercrest Nursing Home (extra credit to go on my otherwise shaky transcripts), I never would have gone geriatric. In my suburban wasteland (Vevey, Iowa, pop. 5,646), I was easily bored by the child-women that buzzed and clucked around me, hugging their transistor radios to their impatient, sweatered breasts. But at the nursing home, repeating my name, changing the channel, listening to the foxtrot tales ("I was a very good dancer, young man, cha-cha-cha"), I learned to love the slight chemical smell and chicken skin of the grandmother-women. While the other boys sneaked off to read *Playboy* and *Penthouse* in the bathroom, I pored over *Modern Maturity* and the *Saturday Evening Post*.

Ladies and gentlemen of the jury, exhibit one is the box behind the lawn mower in the garage: there my Colita lies in state, packed like frozen lamb chops in a six-foot container of dry ice and liquid nitrogen. I had her stored away for a rainy day, when the scientists can thaw her out and fit her back together.

Because Colita Robinson is stone dead and in a million pieces.

It had begun with an uncomfortable, ill-fated romance at the Clayton Agricultural College. Doreen Robinson was a fertilizer major who always had about her the faint rank smell of her chosen field. I met her in the school cafeteria where she was carrying her tray to one of the Formica-topped tables that had all the charm of a fast-food joint that had inspired its design. It's true that Doreen had a pretty face with a Betty Page cut and a full, rambunctious bosom. But what I noticed first was the copy of *Golden Age* magazine ("For the Jet-Set Retiree") haphazardly rolled up on her tray.

"Good read?" I said, joining her at her table.

"What? Oh, *this*." She hacked out a cigarette laugh. "No, that's just got for Gramma. She lives with us in the back. She's a pain in the ass, but, you know—family."

I nodded in a feigned gesture of sympathy. "How old is she?"

"*God,* I dunno. She must be in her eighties now. She's really up there."

"Married?"

"What?" Doreen emitted her trucker laugh again. "I just *got* here. I'm eighteen!"

"No, your grandmother," I said.

That Friday I took Dore to the movies, a stale confection about a dog with supernatural powers. I already knew from our inaugural meeting that Doreen's gramma lived in a converted barn at the back of her driveway. As I escorted Dore into my Chevy Impala I glimpsed the old bat peering though the curtains in her Rockwellian dollhouse. A fluorescent light behind her bathed her unkempt gray hair in a frosted halo, and I couldn't help noticing that her shocking pink lipstick was smudged and one of her eyelashes had fallen off.

It was love at first sight.

"Oh, that's Nana Co." Doreen smiled and waved at her gramma, who waved blankly back. "She's a bit . . ." Doreen spun her finger in the international symbol for *bonkers*.

"She looks pretty," I offered.

Doreen coughed out a laugh. "She has her days. Give her a box of Poppycock and she's eating out of your hand."

A few days later I turned up at the barn. It was mid-afternoon, when I knew Dore had a seeding seminar. I rapped on the door. In my left hand was the latest issue of *Golden Age* magazine. In my right hand was a box of the caramel popcorn known as Poppycock.

I rapped again.

Finally I heard shuffling and the door opened a crack. "Whashoo want?" I could see that Colita's dentures had been haphazardly jammed in her mouth, and she was chewing on them, trying to get them in place.

"I'm Doreen's friend," I said. "Hubert."

"Sheesh noshere."

"I know. She wanted me to give you the new *Golden Age*." I held up the magazine for her to inspect. But I noticed she was eyeing the Poppycock.

"Yoosh besher come insh," she said.

Colita's house was as tidy as the room-furnishings department at the local Wal-Mart. The small round table in the kitchenette was already set (for one) and the radio was on. She was listening to Rush Limbaugh.

"Here, I brought you this." I offered up the crunch.

"Shansh," she said dully. She took the box and plonked it on the table. "I shoon eesh the shtuff." She pointed a shaky finger at her mouth. "It gesh shuck in my *teesh*."

We chatted a bit about the weather and the paucity of senior-citizen discounts. From my days at Rivercrest I knew how to draw old people out, to find their soft spots, as it were. Conversing with Colita, I quickly discovered an obsession with the actor Adam

West, the original TV Batman. (Later I was to discover this interest extended to other superhero figures as well as male ballet dancers—or generally any man in tights.)

"Have you ever seen *The Young Philadelphians*? He's great in that." (I here thanked my photographic memory of obscure film biographies, recalling that West was also in *The Happy Hooker Goes to Hollywood*.)

Colita's smoky eyes briefly lit up. "Thash a goosh film." She patted her mouth, trying to push in her bottom lip. "Cush you ex-scoosh me pleesh?"

She was in the bathroom for over forty-five minutes. At first I heard some gurgling and spitting and then silence for a while, and then a low drone that I gradually realized was snoring.

I waited on the couch, flipping through *Golden Age,* admiring the foundation-garment ads. When the door unclicked, I looked up to see Colita emerge from the bathroom. She was wearing a pink see-through nightie that barely covered her thighs and pink fluffy slippers. She was nude underneath.

"Nana Robinson," I said. "I think you're trying to seduce me."

A few weeks went by and Colita and I began seeing more and more of each other. I bought her little gifts: picture books on Nureyev and Superman, a sporty metal walker, new dentures.

Doreen was puzzled why I kept missing her, leaving notes for under her door: "Sorry I came by at the wrong time. Had a nice visit with Gramma." And "Too bad you were out. Nana Co and I watched *The Rockford Files*." I didn't want to keep my friendship with her grandmother a secret. I thought it might lessen the blow when it finally came.

It didn't.

"You *what?*"

"We want to get married," I said. Nana Co smiled at me. We were sitting on her couch, holding hands.

"Is this some kind of joke?" said Doreen. She was on her third Marlboro.

"No joke," I said. "We're driving to Vegas in the morning."

"The Graceland Chapel," said Colita with a girlish laugh. She sounded a lot better with her new dentures. "They have an Elvis impersonator who does the service."

Doreen exhaled an angry ribbon of smoke. Then she reached for the phone.

If Doreen hadn't told the police that I was planning to kidnap her grandmother, we would have kept to our schedule. But the unexpected circumstances—a police cruiser headed our way— forced me to fight off Doreen as I dragged Colita out of the barn and into the driveway, practically throwing her into the Impala. We could hear the jagged pierce of the police siren as we made our getaway and speeded off to Route 90.

For six weeks we crisscrossed the midwest, Indiana to Kansas, Oklahoma to New Mexico. We had to postpone the Vegas wedding as we assumed Doreen had alerted the authorities there to be on the lookout for us. So we lived from motel to motel, posing as grandmother and grandson.

Colita Robinson was sprightly for an eighty-seven-year-old. Her alligator skin was the color of parchment, but the sex was good—slow and careful, with frequent breaks for Ben-Gay and Extra-Strength Tylenol. I called her "Co" or "Cola." She called me "Poppy."

We found a sweet little gingerbread home in Arthur, Nebraska, became like an old married couple, satiated and bored. We stopped having sex, except occasionally after watching an old Superman episode on TV, or if the local PBS station did *Swan Lake*.

Then, one morning, everything changed. Colita was the first to notice the car that had been shadowing us to and from the local CVS where we picked up Co's many prescriptions. Improbably for a private investigator, the car was a lime green VW Passat, but its ubiquity wherever we went clearly signified its identity. We waited till the middle of the night before packing our belongings in the car and taking off.

We drove three hundred miles to Norton, Kansas, where we spent two nights at the Sincerity Motel. Then I thought I caught sight of a green Passat outside an IHOP, so we left the lodge and drove eighty miles to Hill City.

Being on the run had the effect of reigniting our passion. While pretending to admire the landscape, Co would slip a shrunken, gnarled hand onto my lap and burrow it into my crotch, all the while sweetly singing "99 Bottles of Beer on the Wall." By the eighty-second bottle, I would have stopped by another motor lodge and we'd have another bout of mechanical mid-afternoon sex.

That's how we'd come to Jenson, Colorado, where I finally relented to Co's fervent entreaty to alter my bedroom attire. Shedding my shoes and socks, my pants and shirt and my boxers, I stepped into a pair of sheer white tights. Co's jaw dropped and the bottom plate of her dentures fell out.

"Fush," she said.

Six hours later I was awoken by guttural snoring. Co was passed out across the bare mattress. I was naked, slick with sweat; the sheets and blankets lay on the floor in a clump next to what I thought at first was a pile of bandages. It was the tights, torn to shreds. I blindly reached for the water on the night table and almost took a swig until I heard a clink, and looked down to see Colita's dentures swirling at the bottom of the glass.

I needed some air. And I needed a drink.

I went out in search of a bar, but all the town had to offer was an old duckpin bowling alley with a liquor license.

I went in and ordered a double Jameson's.

It was awhile before, in my addled state, I even noticed the man who had taken the stool next to mine.

"Do you have the Geritol time?" he asked.

"The what?"

"The time? Have you the time?"

"Sorry. I thought you said something else." I pointed out the neon clock on the wall over the Miss Bowling Alley of 1986 calendar.

"Thank you," the man said. "Name's Wilty."

"Hello," I said curtly.

He motioned to the bartender. "A cola for me. I could use a nice, cold cola—and a smile."

And I saw now that he was smiling at me, horrifically—he had braces clutching yellow teeth, and a small greasy Ernie Kovacs mustache. He could have been anywhere from thirty-four to sixty.

"Do you like cola, Mr. . . . ?"

"It's fine," I said impatiently. "Though it seems smarter to ask for a more specific brand."

"Oh, I think cola's quite specific enough for me. I like cola well enough. Though perhaps mine doesn't go quite as easy down the throat as yours does."

I punched him hard in the jaw, knocking him off his stool.

"Hey!" the bartender yelled. "Take it outside!"

Wilty looked up, startled, rubbing his chin. When he stood up I noticed how small he was—barely five-foot-six—and he was wearing red suspenders. He perched himself back on his stool. "Allow me to properly introduce myself. I am Curtis Wilby, Private Investigator. I represent a certain Doreen Robinson who I believe is missing her grandmother."

"What of it?"

"We—that is, I—have reason to believe she has been kidnapped. That you might be familiar with her whereabouts."

"I don't know what you're talking about."

"Ah, well, you see I think you do."

I reached for my whiskey and, in the clink of the ice cube, was suddenly reminded of Colita's dentures. I put the glass back down on the bar.

"What do you want, Mr. Wilty?"

"I have been instructed to offer you fifty thousand dollars for the safe return of a certain elderly woman."

"Doreen wants to buy back her grandmother?"

"She wants what's best for her grandmother, which isn't with you. She thinks you're sick."

"She wants to put Doreen in a home."

"When can I see her? Now would be fine."

I thought of Co passed out on the bed, the sheets in a pile on the floor, the torn white tights in a clump.

"Not now," I said.

"When then?"

"Tomorrow. Here at noon. You'll see she's in fine shape. She's happy with me."

"We'll see. And don't try to skip town. I'm *this* far from calling the police." He held up his fingers, showing how far he was from such a call. It looked like about two inches.

When I got back to the motel I started packing. Colita groggily looked up from the bed.

"Warsh you doonsh?"

"We're leaving. This place is giving me the creeps." I scooped up the clothes on the floor and shoved them into a suitcase. "And for godsake put your dentures in!"

We drove six hundred miles to Wilcox, Arizona, settling in a retirement village next to an old amusement park. For twelve hours a day the windows rattled from the clickity-clack of the rickety wooden roller-coaster, as teenagers squealed and laughed. Inside, geriatric neighbors shuffled past our door, whispering about the odd couple in Room 309. I was beginning to feel stifled, trapped in an airless world, weary of humoring Co's infatuation with Adam West, and tired of her ignorance of any music after Dinah Shore. Also, I was sick of Rush Limbaugh, whom Colita listened to on the radio for the show's full three interminable hours of bloviation every afternoon. "He knows what he's talking about," she'd say after hearing another paean to the low-tax, high-defense-contract, gun-nut crowd. "He's got it all worked out."

It happened while we were shopping at that monstrous retail Kremlin known as Wal-Mart. We were there ostensibly to look for a picnic basket, but became distracted by the severe, militaristic aisles platoon-packed with junk cuisine. We had different tastes in this area; I was partial to the palate-sticking English toffee cookies whereas Colita was searching for her beloved Poppycock, so we were in different aisles at the time of her collapse. I heard a slight crash but thought nothing of it. Eventually, unsuccessful in my savory search, I walked around to her aisle and there she was, sprawled inelegantly across the floor, boxes of caramel popcorn scattered around her. I ran over to her and grabbed her wrist.

"Poppy . . ." she said, fainting, and then her pulse stopped. She was dead.

The rest of the day is a blur to me now. I must have called the cryonics center, because a few hours later my Colita was in ice packs and wrapped in Mylar and we were heading for St. Louis. It was there that Trans Life, Inc. ("Earthly Extension Through Cryonic Suspension"), was located, and I had her transferred to a more suitable traveling casket, a six-foot silver streamline box that resembled a torpedo—or perhaps a huge metallic condom.

Cryonic suspension involves freezing the body shortly after death and keeping it at a temperature of minus 320 degrees Fahrenheit. The temperature can be maintained either by packing the body in an insulated container of dry ice or by covering it in tin foil and immersing it in liquid nitrogen. The theory is that because the body's interior organs are preserved in what is essentially a comatose state, the person can be brought back to life when medical knowledge is at a more advanced state. It is assumed that such common killers as cancer, heart disease, and AIDS will be eventually completely eradicated.

Colita and I had discussed the possibility of freezing her "should any complications arise during our earthly life together," and in anticipation of this, she had transferred some of her money into my Kansas City bank account. She never told me how much it was, but I later discovered it to be somewhere north of 600,000 dollars. In addition, she had left me some real estate in Northern California, 350 acres of a once nondescript, formerly worthless enclave known as Napa Valley.

The cryonics services came to 54,000 dollars, and I decided to look for a small house where Colita and I could settle down until thawing time.

I found a small, single-bedroom home in Summit, Utah, and converted the downstairs living room into Colita's room, placing the box by the TV set where we watched old *Batman* DVDs and listened to Rush Limbaugh in the afternoons. I had the Impala customized, removing the front passenger seat and half the backseat, so by placing Colita's box at an angle, and strapping it in with two pairs of seat belts (fore and aft), it held snugly as long as I kept to a reasonable speed. On weekends I'd take her out for excursions, disguising the receptacle under a tablecloth, posing it as a family-sized picnic box. There was a lot of parkland in the area, and as I ate corn on the cob and cheese sandwiches, I'd read her gossip items from the *Summit Telegram*.

As part of Trans Life's expanding empire, a cryonics outlet was opened on the edge of town a year later, and I occasionally ran Cola up there for checkups. The engineers plugged her body into various machines as I held her frozen hand, looking down on her stilled, breathless corpse. With the right makeup—a smother of pancake, some smudged lipstick—she looked almost alive, just on the other edge of sleeping, and I'd lean down and kiss her softly on her stone-cold lips. An engineer consulting a screen would look over at us, touched.

"You really loved your grandmother, didn't you?"

Then one day, on our way back from a leisurely afternoon at Mayfield Park, as I was speeding down a Route 7 unblemished by traffic while listening to a Dinah Shore CD, I noticed a police cruiser trailing us in the fast lane. I quickly picked up speed, jamming my foot on the accelerator and swerving around cars, trying to lose the cruiser. I had visions of Doreen summoning the entire western police fleet, tracking my every move, trying to steal my Colita away from me.

I spotted a dirt road jutting out from the highway at a sharp angle on the right, and I quickly swerved around to the side. As I was making the turn, the side door of the Impala flew open, and to my horror I watched as the silver torpedo began gently slipping out of the car. I swerved again, attempting to glide the box back in, but it just slithered out onto the highway, bumping across the lanes, tumbling over and over until the lid broke off, and Colita, my Cola, my Co, was floating across the stretch of the roadway, floating in slow-ow motion like a horrific instant replay, and my eyes burned as I watched my Colita, my Cola, my Co, dressed in a white house-coat and plastic slippers, bumping, skipping, and *smashing* into a thousand little pieces on the terrible tarmac of the highway.

I was booked for speeding, resisting arrest (I vaguely remember trying to punch a highway patrolman), and littering state-owned property. It turned out that all the cop wanted to do was get home in time to see a popular TV show involving contestants who battled alligators while answering insipid sports trivia questions (it was the semifinals). With my clean record and guilty plea, I got off with a reprimand and a three-hundred-dollar fine.

True, I was lucky. Doreen didn't seem to hear or care about the accident, and Wilty was apparently off the case. Myself, I was dumbfounded, my mind a clutter of pieces. I had tried to pick them all up, throwing them back into the box of dry ice, but Trans Life said it was hopeless, especially with some of the pieces missing. I went back to the highway a few times looking for them—a finger here, a few toes by the trees, other pieces that could have been any-thing (stones? animal parts?)—but I never found them all. What I did collect is stored in the torpedo of liquid nitrogen, packed in the garage behind the lawnmower.

With the sale of the Napa Valley property, I have a comfortable life. I've stopped running. I listen to Rush Limbaugh and watch reruns of the *Lawrence Welk Show*. And I've started volunteering again, putting in a few hours a week at the local nursing home. Especially Tuesdays. That's polka night.

ERNEST SHACKLETON

OBDURANCE

With Amundsen's successful conquest of Lewisham (by way of a cunning route, taking the Wapping Line to New Cross Gate and then catching a 36 straight down Lewisham Way), I set out on a far different and, if I may say so, dangerous expedition: to sail single-handedly around London in a twenty-six-foot sloop. This, unfortunately, was deemed too difficult, as a large trench would have had to be dug into the Ring Road and then flooded. I decided then to go south, to cross the difficult, largely unchartered terrain of South London on foot and occasional public transportation. I would traverse all the way from Vauxhall to Woolwich, and I would do so single-handedly with fourteen other men.

Amundsen may have won Lewisham for Norway (or is it Sweden?), but I was damned if I was going to let the whole of Southeast London be claimed by a Scandinavian. Many people urged me to reconsider this dangerous expedition, especially after the loss of Scott somewhere in SE11 (he was last seen on a 159 heading down towards Brixton).

The newspapers were then filled with unhappy news. Readers will recall the tense national situation at the time of our launch. David Beckham had been reported drinking late into the evening and had smashed several mirrors at Stringfellows. In addition, the royal family was embroiled in a number of scandals, including Princess Anne being stopped for speeding on the M4. It was a difficult time for all of us. How important really was a crossing of Southeast London when the whole world seemed mad and on the brink of almost certain uncertainty?

Chapter One

We set off from Whitehall with fourteen men and twenty-six dogs. The crowds that day were inspiring, waving flags and cheering us along.

"Weather looks good, sir," said Cutter, my First Mate. I looked up and indeed it was a glorious day; the sky was unblemished of clouds.

We waited at the stop outside the Boots pharmacy. A few minutes later a 36 came by and the door opened. I ushered my party onboard.

"No dogs," said the conductor.

"What?"

"Sorry, Gov—no dogs on the bus."

Here was our first setback—and we hadn't even gone anywhere.

We abandoned the dogs and got on the bus. Midshipman Bates paid while I checked the supplies. I could hear the dogs whimpering and couldn't bear to look back at them. Then I heard Cutter's voice and what he said cheered me immeasurably: "Look, a geezer's giving 'em some chips."

It was smooth sailing past Westminster—the wind carried us up St. Margaret Street and along Millbank and we got across the Thames with no problem. The boys cheered as we crossed the Bridgefoot and approached Vauxhall.

Then the bus unaccountably turned away from the scheduled route of Harlyford Road and headed up Kennington Lane.

"What's this?" I inquired of the conductor.

"Roadwork, Gov. We're being rerouted to Lambeth."

Luckily I had brought with me a bus map. A good leader plans for just such an event. I consulted with Cutter. "We can change at Lambeth North."

Cutter looked out the window at the threatening sky. "I don't know, sir. It doesn't look very cricket out there."

"We'll be fine," I said.

Then, just before the juncture of Lambeth Road and St. Georges Road, we had our third setback of the day: the bus broke down.

"Sorry, folks—everyone off!" said the conductor. "This bus is out of service!"

We all got off and set our provisions on the pavement. I looked over and saw that we were just outside the Imperial War Museum. This was indeed fortuitous as we could get something to eat. I sent Midshipman Peters into the museum to get some sandwiches while Cutter and I looked at the map and assessed our situation. Either we could wait for a 10 or walk the short distance to Elephant & Castle, a depressing roundabout open to the elements and situated around an ugly, mysterious metal structure the purpose of which no one knew. But it was a major transportation hub and it increased our options manyfold. We could either catch a 12 or 171 outside the tube station, following Scott's route to Camberwell, or we could try for a 53, picking up Amundsen's route at the bottom of the Old Kent Road. The problem with this latter choice was the unreliability of the 53. But then the 12 or 171 routes came with their own perils; though more dependable than the 53, either one would take us out of our way, and there was always a lot of traffic on Kennington Park Road. In addition, it had started to rain. This did not bode well for catching a bus; they tended to fill up as soon as the weather turned sinister.

"I say we go for a 53," said Cutter.

I patted him on the back. "You're a good man, Cutter."

I announced our decision to the group. The men cheered.

But Peters still hadn't returned from the museum. My stomach filled with knots. We waited another fifteen minutes, but Peters still hadn't appeared, and it was starting to turn dark. Should we have left him and pressed on? I tell you, the thought never crossed my mind.

"I'm going in," I said.

Cutter persuaded me that I would be of more use staying with the main party and guarding the provisions. He suggested we send Robertson and Lund to find Peters; they were young and had experience in museums from their many years in the Boy Scouts. We sent them in, each carrying a rucksack with Maltezers and fake student cards.

It was a tense ten minutes.

Finally we spotted the three of them at the top of the building's steps, behind the two battleship guns in the forecourt. A loud cheer went up from the party, and much slapping on the backs of the men as they rejoined us.

"He was down in the Trench Experience," said Robertson.

Peters looked sheepish. And there were no sandwiches.

"Sorry, sir."

"What's in the sack?" I demanded of him, noticing that he was holding a small IWM bag.

Peters took out a CD of *The Best of Vera Lynn*. He explained that he had accidentally gone to the gift shop instead of the cafeteria and then got lost down in the exhibits.

For the first time I questioned my judgment in the men I had chosen to take with me on this arduous journey. We would need better wits about us if we were to endure on the difficult road ahead.

As we gathered our provisions for the trek to the Elephant, I noticed a box of Crunchies missing. I assembled the group and informed them of this unexpected deficit. A shaky hand went up. It was Pollak.

"Yes, Pollak."

"I ate 'em, sir."

"You ate an entire box of Crunchies between Westminster and Lambeth?"

"Yes, sir. Sorry, sir. I couldn't wait for the sandwiches, and Peters was taking ever such a long time."

I was very cross. But a leader does not instill confidence in his men by making them fear him. If we were to meet this challenge, we would all need to trust each other. It was time to press on to the Elephant.

Chapter Two

By the time we reached the Elephant & Castle, it was nightfall and the rain was whipping down hard on our backs. I was sorry now that I'd had our provisions wrapped in cardboard instead of wood. I noticed Harwood struggling under the weight of a great box.

"What have you got there, Harwood?"

"It's the dog food, sir."

"Dash it, man—we don't need the dog food anymore. Drop it on the side there and help Fletcher with the sousaphones."

"Yes, sir."

There was a large crowd at the bus stop, and after we had failed to get on four buses in a row, I decided it best to set up camp for the night and try in the morning.

It was a long, cold night. We lit a fire in a litter bin, and some of the men began singing old Negro spirituals as we passed around photographs of our pets. I thought of the cheering crowds we'd left at Westminster and then I thought of the dogs we'd had to leave behind.

I told Cutter how I missed little Gladstone, my dachshund.

"Oh, he's all right, I'm sure," said Cutter. "He never did like the cold and rain. It would have been a hard journey for him. And he always did like chips."

"Yes, chips. Thank you, Cutter. You are a decent chap."

"I'm not sure the poodles would have been very useful either, sir."

Chapter Three

The morning greeted us with a tentative sunshine. I told Cutter I'd had a fretful night, awoken once an hour by a loud, blurry red vision that passed us on the street.

"That would be the night busses," he said.

"Night busses?" I'd forgotten about the N53. We'd slept through six opportunities to move on. We folded up the tents and equipment. I sent Perkins in for a newspaper. He came out with the *Telegraph,* his face ashen.

"What is it?"

He handed me the paper. It was grim news indeed—Prince William had been arrested again for shoplifting. I assembled the group and told them of the situation.

"I don't want any of you to continue if you feel your heart is no longer in it. I understand that the country is on the brink of madness, that the national situation has catastrophe written all over it. I would not think the lesser of you if you elected to turn back and join your loved ones in this time of questionable sanity. But anyone who chooses the other way—the longer way, the tougher way, the way of the Obdurance Expedition—then step forward."

To a man, they stepped forward. I tell you, I felt a lump in my throat and wiped a tear from my face.

"Good chaps," I squeaked. "I will say only that I am glad you are not a bunch of scared little girls. It would be no good to have little pinkie poofters along. We wouldn't have had your party dresses anyway, and what would you do without your lipsticks . . . ?"

Cutter gave me a look.

"Yes, well . . . Let's press on."

We waved down a 177 and carried the provisions on the bus. Foster was struggling with the printing equipment, which included a new letterhead press and a crate of twelve alphabet fonts. I helped him with encouragement: "Pick it up a bit, Foster, there's a chap." We were forced to sit upstairs as the lower deck was completely full. Everyone was reading about the latest royal problems and the current marmalade crisis.

We had a clear shot on the Old Kent Road, straight down past Millwall to New Cross Gate. We saluted as we passed the marker of Amundsen's base camp where they'd been forced to eat a couple of their dogs.

We were now in Deptford and I made a fateful decision: to stop in at Buster's for some jellied eels.

It was not long before I almost lost four men (Payson, Tutor, Waldron, and Phipps), who became violently ill with what I can only assume was some kind of "food poisoning." We left them in the gents, retching into the lavatories. "Don't stay . . . on our account . . . sir," said Peters haltingly, staring into a toilet.

"I quite agree with you, Jones."

"Peters."

"Yes, Peters. We must forge ahead. But I *will come back* for you. You look like you've lost your lunch. Here's a fiver—buy yourself and the others another round of eels."

"Uhhhhhhh," Peters replied, spewing forthwith into the commode.

Chapter Four

The ten of us of hardier stock stood by Nunhead Cemetery. I had planned to catch a 272 to Blackheath, but there was a long wait, and no omnibus appeared. "What's the problem?" I said. "There should be one every twelve minutes."

"That's the weekday schedule," said Cutter.

Weekday schedule! What poor planning!

We traversed the cemetery to find a shortcut to Catford, where I hoped we might make another connection. But by the time we reached the other end of the park we were greeted by the unfortunate discovery that all the exits were locked after 6:00 P.M. We therefore had to double back to our starting point for the day—a loss of several hours. By then it was nightfall and rather than stumble about in the dark I decided to set up camp.

As a diversion I had the men take out the printing press and publish a special edition newspaper. Thus was born the *Obdurance Gazette,* Issue One. James interviewed me for an exclusive report, and Bates produced some fine illustrations of our expedition so far. Robertson wrote a leader congratulating us on our mission, and Harwood created a comic strip called "Shackeltoon" (very amusing), while Fletcher and Sitwell produced a crossword puzzle—preventing anyone from getting any sleep—but it was well worth it, and the sixteen-page special edition was sold out in six minutes, forcing us to go into a second printing. Unfortunately, Sitwell got a finger stuck in a press and Lund had to amputate it with a trench fork. It was a messy job, and Lund grabbed what he thought was a second-edition *Obdurance Gazette* to staunch the bleeding. It turned out to be the bus map. It was ruined and we were now, to all intents and purposes, blind. Southeast London is forbidding terrain, and we'd have to feel our way north as best we could with a compass.

We found the Brockley Rise and climbed our way back to Deptford where, as luck would have it, Peters, Tutor, Phipps, and Waldron were sitting in a laundrette, waiting for their clothes to dry. Tutor was reading the morning's *Daily Mail,* which bore the shocking news of the theft of Elton John's 1947 Bentley. I said a prayer, and when the Deptford group's clothes were dry, we headed east towards Blackheath.

Chapter Five

On the crossroads of Blackheath Road and Lewisham Way we had the great good fortune to run into an old friend: the 53. We boarded the omnibus to find it completely empty, affording us the ability to sit downstairs with our twenty-seven crates of equipment. As a treat I had the men break open the box of Mars bars and we all had a good snack.

There was a hard rain, and the men took refuge in the National Maritime Museum. I went out to Trafalgar Road to look for a cab. I confess I had little hope of finding a taxi in Greenwich in the rain, and indeed none was forthcoming. I fell then on the fateful decision of proceeding alone, to make it as best I could back to the West End to summon help for the rest of the party.

I went out in search of the mythical foot tunnel to the Isle of Dogs. A short walk to the High Street afforded me an astounding discovery: the Docklands Light Railway system that I had thought ended at Island Gardens across the Thames now continued southward, through Greenwich itself, and all the way to Lewisham! I therefore had a clear shot on the tube to Monument where I could catch the District Line straight to Westminster.

Word of my return must have preceeded me (or so I believed), for when I stepped out of the station opposite Parliament, there were already huge crowds clogging the streets all the way up to Trafalgar Square. It turned out to be a welcome for the British badminton team which had just defeated Brazil in the world championship, 2-0.

Weary and hungry (though admittedly cheered by the badminton win), I stumbled into the Travellers Club on Pall Mall just after 7:00 P.M. In the Smoking Room, the men in leather armchairs stared at me dumbfoundedly.

"Shackleton—we thought you were dead!" said Lord Ashby, whom we all called Tootles.

"No, I was in Greenwich. I found a southeast passage under the Thames from the Isle of Dogs."

"Yes, the Docklands Light Railway. Nifty, eh?"

"So you knew about this?"

"Oh yes, that's been running for years."

I told Tootles about my men stuck at the National Maritime Museum, that I'd promised I'd return to fetch them.

"Don't worry, they'll all be flushed out at closing time," said Tootles confidently. "They can take the tube back."

There was a shriek from the other side of the room.

"What is it?" I asked.

The man, a new member I wasn't acquainted with, was ashen-faced. "It's terrible news," he answered. "Scott has been found in Devon."

"Is he dead?"

"No, he's running a sweet shop in Polperro."

"But that's excellent news," I said.

"Yes, but the Duke of Bedford's garage has burned down."

I collapsed in a heap on the rug. Whether it was from exhaustion or the relentless parade of ill news concerning the royal family's petty criminal mishaps and the incendiary nature of their possessions, I can't be sure.

When I awoke I was in a private room at Guys Hospital, surrounded by all fourteen members of the Obdurance Expedition, alive and well.

"Reporting to duty, sir," said Cutter.

"Excellent work, men," I said, quickly wiping a tear from my face.

"What's next, sir?"

And I told them of my next plan, an excursion not even the newly alive Scott had attempted: to follow the circumference of Queen Mary's Gardens in Regent's Park—counterclockwise and on foot! I'm pleased to report that they all signed up—except for Fletcher who said he had a Yoga class.

VIRGINIA WOOLF

WILLIAM POWELL DIARY
(1936)

February 28.   *Mrs. William Powell*
          Virginia Stephens Powell
          Mrs. Virginia Powell
          Mrs. Virginia Woolf-Powell

My life for a "Thin Man." Leonard is more skeletal than thin. He says we must tighten our belts if we are to survive the winter.

No reply from my letter to W.P. Perhaps other people have already pointed out the myriad inconsistencies in *The Great Ziegfeld*—the film's manufacturers violated their own conceit by creating a long scene that took up a huge amount of space, and yet was ostensibly set on a theatre stage that was *much too small* to house this sequence. My God, there were *swimming pools* the size of Grosvenor Square— an incredible supposition.

The papers are full of the Abdication crisis. The King looked very lost in the newsreels, his eyes vacant and confused.

Can't help thinking of Powell's delightful little moustache. Why can't W.P. be our King? I'd vote for him!

March 1. Vita has been pestering me to come down to Sissinghurst again. How gardens do bore me! Perhaps I should visit New York, apply for a job with Jed Harris & work for the Theatre Guild. Or Hollywood? H.G. Wells did some scriptwriting work and he said it was ridiculously easy. They put you up in a cabin and supply you with an office and a "broad" who does all the typing (and other sundry errands that Wells didn't go into). You literally recite the script, and the "broad" takes it down like dictation. Question: Could I get a "broad" to transcribe my novels?

The new factotum, a boy L. and I picked up at the orphanage for four pounds, is v. slow. I think I saw him playing with the dirty laundry from the hamper (or was that Quentin?).

If I went to Hollywood, of course there's always the possibility I'd be invited to a party at a mansion in the Hollywood Mountains and I could meet W.P.

March 4. Curses! According to *Screen World,* W.P. is being seen "about town" with Jean Harlow, the silver-haired harlot. What can he possibly see in her? She has the mouth of a lorry driver and the grace of a chicken. Oh William, William . . . Surely a middle-aged, married English novelist with a history of mental instability is more your type.

March 10. L. said the plumbing at Monks House needs replacing, & we must collect money for the International Brigade to fight fascism in Spain. Oh sod the International Brigade! I want to foxtrot cheek-to-cheek with William Powell in the Rainbow Room at Rockefeller Centre. I want to be a jewel thief. I want to dance dance dance! G.B. Shaw can go stick a firecracker up his own bum for all I care!

March 11. Well, I got a little carried away yesterday apparently. L. said he found me dancing with a tree in the rain last night, singing "Hooray for Hollywood." I don't remember any of it. Woke at 11 A.M. with such a headache, and have been bedridden all day. Could have sworn I heard one of the sparrows in the garden tell me to kill L. and go to Pittsburgh. But why Pittsburgh? Why not Chicago? Or Hollywood?

L. has just come in with some tea & soup. What a dear, sweet thing he is. Vaguely remember hitting him on the head with one of the fireplace tongs. Could I really have done that? But if I didn't, what accounts for the huge bruise on his forehead? And why else would he keep me tied to the bedstead?

March 15. Of course! W.P. was born in Pittsburgh.

March 18. Good news: Jean Harlow is dead. (Did W.P. kill her?) The sparrows have been giving me messages again: "Stab Leonard with a pencil & take the Normandie to New York." (Or did I get that wrong? But "Stab Normandie with Leonard and take a pencil to New York" doesn't make any sense. Or should I stab a pencil and take *Leonard* to New York? But what of Normandy? *The sparrows are idiots.*) L. has in fact been v. understanding, esp. considering I tried to kill him twice with a pair of scissors before breakfast. But why is he trying to keep me away from W.P.? Why does he destroy all of W.P.'s letters to me?

March 23. Tom Eliot over for lunch with his loony wife, Vivian. I think I saw her trying to eat a copy of *Mrs. Dalloway* (or was that Quentin?). Tom is v. clever but such a bore. He really does act like a vicar sometimes. We were having a perfectly decent conversation about Roger Frye's obsession with Shirley Temple, & suddenly Tom starts speaking in Latin! Or at least it sounded like Latin. What could I do in a situation like that but start hitting him with L.'s tennis racket? Woke up several hours later & found myself tied to the bed again. Am beginning to think this tied-to-the-bed thing of L.'s is becoming something of a trope.

March 30. Letter from Vita asking me down to Knole. "Who is this William Parnell you keep on about?" she writes. Such a thick-headed dolt! She has no idea who King Vidor is either ("Is he the one in charge in Abyssinia now?") No wonder the sun is setting on the British Empire. Tried to hit L. with a billiard stick. He was v. nice about it and chained me up in the coal shed. A little while later he came by with some Eccles cakes & a cup of tea. Such a sweet man.

April 4. Is William Powell trying to reach me? At the post office, when I asked for my "secret Hollywood letters" that L. has been withholding from me, the clerk gave me a very odd stare. Something is definitely up. Saw a man on Charing Cross Road with W.P.'s lovely little moustache and followed him all the way to High Holborn, where he alerted a constable. But why would the man steal W.P.'s moustache? Must get it back for him and deliver it in person.

Question: Could I get L. to grow a moustache and then cut it off so I could bring it to W.P. in Hollywood? Would L. agree to this?

April 6. L. says he is finally fed up with my W.P. infatuation and tells me that W.P. doesn't actually exist. Apparently he's played by a fat man from Woodbridge named Burt Hadrian. "His moustache isn't even real," says L. Can this be true? Was the Great Ziegfield really played by a fat man from East Anglia? And how does he look so thin in the pictures? L. says it's all done with special effects. I am very upset by this. Does this mean that Jean Harlow is still alive and actually a charwoman from Hull?

April 10. Feel much better now. Resigned to the fact that there is no W.P. It seems obvious now—a man with a nose like that couldn't possibly be thin or American or real at all.

Went to the pictures to forget my troubles. It was a very silly film about an explorer in Africa who wears a solar topee and has a moustache v. similar to W.P.'s. Much more masculine than W.P. as well. Of course now I know that these Hollywood actors don't actually exist, but as I was coming out of the cinema, I was sure I saw Mr. Gable waiting for me in a taxi. When I got closer he had gone. Mustn't mention this to L., he would just worry. Already the sparrows are on my side and telling me to hit L. with a cricket bat. Of course! Why didn't I think of this before?

NORMAN MAILER

THE RULES: How to Meet Women, Marry Women, Divorce Women, and Meet New Women

As I have a certain record for relationships (I've dated hundreds of women, and married many of them), a publisher of gift books and novelty coffee mugs has asked to put together a small collection of my dating tips. Obviously, you can't learn everything from a book—like any pursuit, practice makes perfect. My overriding advice is: Marry early, and marry often. But here are some tips that might help you along the way:

Never dance on a first date.
Tough guys don't dance. I made this mistake once while on a first date with the Duchess of Argyll—you end up looking foolish and a photo invariably gets into *The Guardian*.

Never meet her halfway or go Dutch on a date.
Again, I've learned from experience. I once went Dutch on a date with Gloria Steinem—and it was a disaster. All she wanted to do was harass me about my supposed male chauvinism and sexist writings. If only I had shown up with flowers and chocolates and taken her to the Russian Tea Room! But it was too late—we went to

Town Hall, where I was jumped by sixteen feminists and beaten to a pulp. Not only that, they filmed the whole thing, and it ended up playing for sixteen weeks at the Beekman and later turned up on Public Television. Talk about humiliation!

Don't open up too fast.

This is good advice. On my first date with Marilyn Monroe I spent seven hours talking about my obsession with her and the therapeutic effects of anal sex. She started looking alarmed, took an overdose of sleeping pills, and excused herself for an early call on *Niagara*. (This puzzled me as the film had already been out for six years.) Let her get a word in edgewise. Listen to her insecurities—you can prey on them later.

An execution is not a good date.

How was I to know? I had two tickets to the Timothy McVeigh Lethal Injection, which the press had made out to seem like the hottest event in town. Imagine my surprise when my date actually threw up in the viewing room, leaving me feeling hurt and embarrassed. Before you go out on a date, always get her views on capital punishment.

Don't get drunk before a talk show appearance.

Say you've been invited on the *Dick Cavett Show* with Janet Flanner and Gore Vidal. Sure, there's a temptation to get drunk beforehand and head-butt Gore in the Green Room. Resist the temptation! You end up looking foolish and it reduces your chances of scoring with Janet.

Don't rush into a drug-addled sex binge.

I did this repeatedly in the 1950s—you meet a chick at Caffe Reggio's or a college reading. You bring her back to your Greenwich Village pad, get stoned, and spend ten days wearing out the bare mattress in an orgy of sex. Sure it's fun *at the time*. But how do you feel when you wake up the next month? The girl is half your age and now she wants you to read her poetry. Does this seem like a smart plan for a mature relationship? No, it doesn't. Keep the sex casual—i.e., no anal on the first date. And no poetry!

Never double-date with a Kennedy.
Sure they're a good drawing card, but they're tough competition.
And terrible drivers.

Don't treat your date like a sparring partner.
Just because you can get her to put on the gloves doesn't mean she
actually wants to fight.

**Slowly involve her in your family and introduce her to
your children.**
If you have more than ten children, it's hard to keep this from a
prospective mate; sooner or later (by reading *Who's Who* or seeing a
documentary), she's going to find out. If your youngest child is older
than your date, don't pretend the kid is your personal trainer or sec-
retary. Honesty is the best policy: you were raped in high school and
left by your wife, who was a crack whore.

**Stop dating her if she wants to be an actress or ballet
dancer.**
It'll never work out—she'll become obsessive and confused, and
end up either in a loony bin or meeting a handsome twenty-four-
year-old stud in her acting class. If you're serious about a chick, get
her pregnant as soon as possible. And hide her shoes.

Don't stab your wife.
Even if she deserves it and has been goading you all night at your
own party. Stabbing does not represent an "existential act," and
people are bound later to hold it against you.

Next! And other rules for dealing with rejection.
You're on the outs with your sixth or seventh wife. Is this the end
of the world? Of course not. There's always another chick. Go on
a lecture tour, join the Actor's Studio, get interviewed by a young
babe from the Fox News Channel or the *Harvard Business Review.*

Don't expect a woman to change or try to change her.
Remember: You never really know a woman until you meet her in
court.

JACK KEROUAC

ON THE BUS

This passage, typed on a six-foot scroll of teletype paper, was an early attempt at what came to be known as "automatic writing" and describes Kerouac's life in New York without a car.

I first started using public transportation when my '38 Chevvy lost a fight with a streetlamp on the Bowery and I felt wary and split-up and that everything was dead. With the end of my car came that part of my life you could call my life on the bus. Before that I'd often thought of driving uptown, often vaguely planning it but never taking off. The bus was the perfect companion for the road because it only cost a nickel and you didn't have to park. Also, it didn't smell as bad as the subway.

I remember taking the M6 from Houston Street to Sixth Ave and then the B12 up to 23rd Street. The city was full of streetlevel jobheads ghostwalking past the flowerbeds of Bryant Park and the dinersmells that scented the soiled air. Wow, I'm getting hungry. When is the Benzedrine gonna kick in? I asked Neal for some paper and all he brings me is this beaten-up piece of teletype paper. I'm beat. Beat like the shaggy dogs of the Wall Street caverns, beat like the junglebeat tom-toms of the African night, beat like my hands on a lonely night in my coldwater flat in Hellskitchen, plus sometimes in the living room, and then maybe in the bathroom. The quick brown fox jumped over the lazy dogg. Hey the g on this Underwood sticks. Ggg. Better avoid all words with g in them. That sentence was okay (except for the g). I sure am hungry. Maybe the benny is kicking in after all. Thinking about that cute Negro chick I met at the Gaslight the other night. Or was it the San Remo? She was a juked-up jazzchick from Harlem and I gave her the sex glance, the do-you-want-to-do-me stare. She seemed to be looking my way, but then she just sneezed in my direction. I wondered what kind of transportation she used, if she took the subway or liked the bus.

Oh yeah, my life on the bus—like the A9 I once took all the way from Bleecker Street to Rockefeller Center, sat next to this big Matahari chick, tried to cop a feel, she looked at me like I was a degenerate or something—me the cool-cat hipster with the square jaw and Hollywood looks and bashful drunken blur. Sometimes I'd miss my stop, have to get out, and have to walk a couple of blocks back to where I was going. Feels weird to be typing nonstop without having to change the papet. I mean paper. Allen's getting kind of chunky these days. I told him to stop eating all those egg rolls. Maybe I should be a homo— everyone else is. Except Neal. Boy is he hot, with that square jaw and Hollywood looks and bashful drunken blur. No wait, I'm straight. Yeah, I'm straight. Gotta take another benny, gotta work this out. Bill is kind of creepy, all he talks about is lost boys in the interzone, strung out on horse. But he's rich, and I like that about him. He asked me to play William Tell with him the other day, shoot an apple off my head. No way, that's how he killed his wife. Still, I was tempted. He said he'd buy me a drink if he missed. Always with the guns already. What am I, Jewish? No, I'm a Canuck. I miss *maman*. Where is she? Remind me to move in with her and become a drunken right-wing Republican. Who am I talking to? This sure is a long piece of teletype paper. Where was I?

Oh yeah, my life on the bus. Those were the crazy years, the wacky years, the zany years. No, not zany—that's too English (tea-cozy scones and crumpet years). Late at night I'd share the bus with cool-cat Negro jazz musicians from 52nd Street and their jazzy broads, blkwingf their horns and chewing on fried chicken drumsticks and cornbread. Boy am I hungry. When's Allen gonna get back with the egg rolls? I could eat a horse.

J. R. R. TOLKIEN

LORD OF THE STRINGS

In the early 1930s, before he completed The Hobbit *and embarked on his vast epic,* The Lord of the Rings, *J. R. R. Tolkien was still formulating his magic world of Middle Earth and had began work on a saga he called "The Lord of the Strings." This ultimately turned out to be a mistaken concept, and it was long thought that he burned the entire five-thousand-page manuscript he'd worked on for many years, to begin anew and more fortuitously with the idea of a magic ring.*

Recently, however, some pages and notes were found in a tea shop in Steep, Hampshire, not far from Tolkien's home. The sheaf of pages (coincidentally tied in string) were marked on the verso with an enigmatic note: "I. O. Stp T. Rm 10/6. J.R.R.T. 11/12/32."

Fellowship of the String

In the westlands of Eradiator, between the Misty Mountains and the District Line, lay Inhibbiton where there lived the gay band of merry inhibbits. Chiefly among them, at little Bog End just across from the tobacconist, was Balbot Biggins, the most inhibbited of the inhibbits, who had for some decades now had in his possession the infamous String of East Mortland.

Balbot was a most intelligent inhibbit, but he was very forgetful. But by using the magic string of East Mortland tied around one of his fingers, he found that he was able to remember things. For instance, he would be at the Tetco in Chetwood, wandering aimlessly up and down the aisles, with no idea what it was he was supposed to be looking for—and then he would look down at his hairy finger, with the piece of yellow string around it, and he would exclaim: "Of course! *Marmite!*"

(Of course, he needed to remember to look at his finger, and so he would put another piece of string on another finger, usually on the other hand, and that would remind him to look at the other string. Or in case he might forget to look at the first string, he would tie other pieces of string on his feet, his elbows, around his nose, and threaded through his eyelashes. As a consequence, Balbot Biggins almost always walked around covered in string—and after a while the string began to lose its significance to him, and it was a permanent feature of his appearance, often just serving to remind him to put on more string—but why, he couldn't, for the life of him, remember.)

And so it was, for many years, until he was getting on in years, though not actually looking much older than Caro Grunt, the famous inhibbited movie star, and he decided that he should leave Inhibbiton and wander the peaks and dales of Medium Earth, so that he might get out of the way for young Flodo to take center stage in the story.

The Two Needles

In the great past of the Olden Years, before the Glandular Glees came down the great Nothern Line by Barnstable, the Two Needles marked the way of the River Ennui. Flodo had by this time passed his driving test, and decided to celebrate by playing Cat's Cradle . . .

Attacked by the Door Locks, Samwhich eats the inedible Bark of Entwok, and is forever hungry. "Can't you pull some strings and get me off this saga?" he asks Flodo.

Bilbo tied up in string? Samwhich accidentally eats string—then vomits magic green map showing positions of discount stores and Lyons Tea Rooms.

Queen of the Flunkies crochets string into magic mittens? (No.)

Flodo must fight the Evil Knitting Needles of East Mortland.

The Return of the Yarn

Gondloff the Mauve produces indestructible suit made out of potholders—but seams come undone, and he's impaled on poisonous crochet hook.

String theory, etc. Flodo tells a good "yarn" (yawn?).

Poppin explains positive use of dental floss to Flodo, so string contains magic power in his teeth?

The Dreaded Hair Shirt of Shagbottom, which causes the Baker's Dozen to get itchy, missing the Grand Medium National.

Flodo and Elrod smoke too much pipe-weed and spend several weeks under some shrubbery, inspecting their fingernails. This allows Saursport to follow their droppings and catch up with them at Durthang Regis. (Big battle with string.) In East Mortland, Flodo has string tied around his finger to remind him to toss string into the bottomless pit of Mount Doom, but he forgets what it's for, and tosses in a jar of Marmite instead—forever dooming all of Medium Earth.

COLE PORTER

YOU'RE FULL OF CRAP

Found among the papers of Wilson Denner (1910–1986), a waiter at the Waldorf-Astoria, these lines were penned by an evidently irate Cole Porter in the late 1930s. The relationship between Denner and Porter is unknown, but the lyrics appear to be a reworking of the composer's famous song "You're the Top," with the conceit interestingly reversed.

You're full of crap
You're the Hindenburg disaster
You're Michelangelo's David (made out of plaster)
I'm a top banana
A Claus that's Santa
I can tap!
But if, Baby, I'm the bestest,
You're full of crap.

You're a prick
You're Hitler's ethics
You're a dick
You're Eddie Cantor's athletics
You're FDR's legs, you're broken eggs
You're Stalinism!

You're a chump
You're Eleanor's voice
You're a dump
In that book by Joyce
You're Lindbergh's baby's killer
You're the pornography of Henry Miller
You're a jolt
But if, Baby, I'm a genius,
You're a dolt.

You're a slime
You're an apple seller
A measly dime from John D. Rockefeller
You're W. C. Fields's liver
You're an Indian giver
You're a fiend
I'd say more but it'd be too obscene.

You're a pest
You're a dog with rabies
You're Chaplin's problem with the young ladies
You're the stock market crash
You're an ist that's Fash
You're a scream
You're a living nightmare, Baby,
But I'm a dream.

You're Chamberlain's accord
You're a broken Ford
In a crash
You closed on opening night
I'm a Broadway smash

You're a freak
You're the Dodgers on a losing streak
I'm the nicest guy
A little shy
But brilliant, too

There's never been enough of me
There's too much of you.

You're Houdini drowned
You're Bing Crosby without sound
Bob Hope with laryngitis
You're a clown
I'm right here but
I'm leaving you at the Lost & Found.

You're the broken-down Munich talks
You're a bunch of bagels without lox
You're a dead stockbroker
A stupid joker
You're a jerk
You have a lousy grin and a stupid smirk.

You're no fun,
you're the R101
You're Picasso in a funk
I'm Hemingway on a sunny day
You're Fitzgerald on a drunk.

You're a bad relation
King Edward after the Abdication
You're a fool
I'm a good example
You're a sample that's a stool.

You're a maniac that's klepto
You're a Marx Brother (but Zeppo)
You're as unemployed as Harold Lloyd
You're a twit
I'd say join the Marines
But you're too unfit.

You're Gary, Indiana, and its vicinity
You're Noel Coward's masculinity

You're Goldwyn's diction
You're science fiction
You're a freak
But if, Baby, I'm a swell guy,
You're a creep.

SAMUEL BECKETT

EN ATTENDANT FRODO

Une rue. Un arbre. Le soir.

ESTRAGON
Où est Frodo?

VLADIMIR
Bof! Tu pense que je sais?

ESTRAGON
J'ai vu Gandalf le Gris hier soir.

VLADIMIR
Vraiment? Comment vas t'il?

ESTRAGON
Il va ça va. Il est très grand, est Gandalf. Avec un grand, er . . .

VLADIMIR
Une barbe?

ESTRAGON

Oui, c'est ça.

VLADIMIR

Je pense que Frodo est très petit.

ESTRAGON

D'accord. Tu sais, j'attends Frodo maintenant.

VLADIMIR

Vraiment? Moi, aussi. Je l'attends pour quelques temps.

ESTRAGON

Frodo—le petit. Il est aussi petit comme un escargot.

VLADIMIR

Un escargot? Je pense il est plus grand que ça.

ESTRAGON

Peut-être. Mais j'ai vu—*je verais*—un escargot très grand qui conduit une voiture.

ESTRAGON

Un SUV?

VLADIMIR

No, un Citroën Deux Chevaux.

ESTRAGON

C'est pas beaucoups des chevaux, deux.

VLADIMIR

C'est pas beaucoups *de tout*. Mais, c'est assez pour un escargot.

ESTRAGON

Je suis d'accord. Sur cet subjet, je suis sur le même page que toi.

VLADIMIR

Merci.

ESTRAGON

De rien.

VLADIMIR

Tu as vu Samwise?

ESTRAGON

L'ami de Frodo?

VLADIMIR

Le même.

ESTRAGON

Pas récemment. *(Une pause)* Je pense que Samwise est peu trop, er . . . *proche* de Frodo.

VLADIMIR

Tu pense?

ESTRAGON

Oui. Je pense quelqu'un pouvait prendre le mal impression des choses entre Frodo et Samwise.

VLADIMIR

Je pense qu'ils sont juste les beaux amis.

ESTRAGON

Si si si. Bien-sûr . . . Mais . . . peut-être c'est pas necessaire de se tenez les mains.

VLADIMIR

Ils se tiennent des mains?

ESTRAGON

De temps en temps.

VLADIMIR
Tu parles.

ESTRAGON
Non, je l'ai vu avec mes mêmes oiseaux.

VLADIMIR
Tes *oiseaux?* Commes les pigeons?

ESTRAGON
Non non non. Je m'excuse. Mes yeux.

VLADIMIR
Ah. C'est different—les oiseaux et les yeux.

ESTRAGON
C'est évident. *(Une pause)* Tu aimes bien Bilbo?

VLADIMIR
Oui. Il est un bon mec. Pourquoi?

ESTRAGON
Pas rien.
(Une pause mala droit)

VLADIMIR
Non, vraiment—dites-moi. Pourqoui demandez-moi?
(Une autre pause)

ESTRAGON
Tu connais le Rialto?

VLADIMIR
Le cinéma dans la rue des Canettes?

ESTRAGON
Le memîme. Alors, un soir je suis allé voir *Je Suis un Fugitif d'un Chain-Gang*.

VLADIMIR

C'est un bon film, ça! Avec le comedian Américain Paul Muni.

ESTRAGON

Oui. Cet film est le mieux.

VLADIMIR

Le mieux? De quoi?

ESTRAGON

Um . . . Cet film est le meilleur film des films d'un certain regard.

VLADIMIR

D'un certain regard de quoi?

ESTRAGON

Têtes-toi! J'essaye te dire de Bilbo!

VLADIMIR

Ah oui. Excusez-moi.

ESTRAGON

Tout ce que! Tiens! Alors. J'étais entrain de voir le film—quand j'ai sense quelque chose . . . sur mes genoux.

VLADIMIR

Qu'est-ce que, les genoux?

ESTRAGON

C'est en haut des jambes.

VLADIMIR

Ah, oui. D'accord. C'est just avant les testicules.

ESTRAGON

Oui. Alors, et je regarde . . . est qui est la, tu pense?

VLADIMIR
Catherine Deneuve?

ESTRAGON
Non. Bilbo Baggins.

VLADIMIR
Zut alors! Mon Dieu! C'est pas vrai!

ESTRAGON
Je promesse, sur la coeur de Charles de Gaulle.

VLADIMIR
C'est extraordinaire! Qu'est-ce que tu as fait?

ESTRAGON
Il était une grande surprise.

VLADIMIR
Bien-sûr. Ça va sans dire.

ESTRAGON
Oui. Alors . . . J'ai pris sa main . . . et l'ai écrasé.

VLADIMIR
Qu'est-ce que, écrasé?

ESTRAGON
Broyer. Er . . . Faire petit *fort* et *vite*.

VLADIMIR
Ah. Oui. Qu'est-ce qu'il as fait?

ESTRAGON
Il était étonné—et en douleur—et je pense qu'il était embaressé.

VLADIMIR
Il est chiant.

ESTRAGON

Comment?

VLADIMIR

Il est une peine dans le derrière.

ESTRAGON

Oui.

VLADIMIR

Et soudainement—il a disparu!

ESTRAGON

Quoi?

VLADIMIR

J'ai eu son main—mais il n'a été pas la!

ESTRAGON

C'est très étrange, n'est-ce pas?

VLADIMIR

Tu me dis! Il est parti! Alor—voilà . . .
   (Il montre un anneau.)

ESTRAGON

Qu'est-que c'est?

VLADIMIR

C'est un anneau.

ESTRAGON

Une bague?

VLADIMIR

Un anneau d'or.

ESTRAGON

Oui, je vois.

VLADIMIR

Tu veux?
  (Une pause)

ESTRAGON

Pourquoi?

VLADIMIR

C'est un peu . . . gay pour moi.

ESTRAGON

Alors, merci beaucoup!

VLADIMIR

Du calme! J'ai pas dit que tu êtes homosexual.

ESTRAGON

Je sais, mai . . . Me le montre encore.
  (VLADIMIR montre l'anneau à ESTRAGON.)

ESTRAGON

C'est pas mal. C'est pas gay de tout.

VLADIMIR

Tu pense?

ESTRAGON

Oui.

VLADIMIR

Alors, je vais le garder.

ESTRAGON

Mais tu veux aller le donner à moi il y a deux secondes!

VLADIMIR

Pas maintenant.

ESTRAGON

Pfff! *(Une pause)* Tu veux attendre à Frodo?

VLADIMIR

Non. Allons-y?

ESTRAGON

Oui, allons-y.
   (Ils vont pas. Fin.)

RAYMOND CARVER

PAPER CUT

The production assistant gave the director a book to read on his trip. She said she thought he might like it. It could be his in-flight reading. The director was flying from London to L.A., a twelve-hour journey. He'd been driving around England scouting locations for a new film. His assistant had to stay behind for more meetings. The director liked England, with its petty eccentricities and good-humored people, but he was glad to be getting back to the U.S.

After the plane had taken off and the pilot had made some muffled pleasantries over the PA system, the director opened his black bag and took out some magazines, production notes, his CD player, and found the book his assistant had given him. He looked down at it curiously. It's not that he never read books, but he didn't do it often. He usually read scripts or just the coverage. He put the book aside and began flipping through the magazines, looking for references to himself or people he knew. Now in his seventies, his world was getting smaller, but he didn't mind. He'd earned the right to a small world.

The airline hostesses fluttered about the passengers in the first-class section. In the quick arithmetic of fame that was automatic to him, the director had calculated that he was the third-most famous person on the plane, after the pop singer and the newscaster. Still, he was surprised at the attention a pretty hostess gave him, flirting with him, squatting in the aisle to chat with him and touch his shoulder. He had to fight the urge to pull the young woman unto his lap.

Vaguely he recalled that they weren't called hostesses anymore. The word *hostess* had become maligned, like so much of the language he'd lived with for so many years. Occasionally he'd say something to people he didn't know very well, and he'd see the color suddenly drain from their faces as an odd, uncomfortable silence seemed to swallow the conversation. It usually happened for just a moment, before the people realized that he didn't know any better, that he was a great film director and he must have been joshing them, surely. He'd have to think back to what it was he'd said that had alarmed them. But really he just didn't give a damn. People should get over it. It was just language, words. And who cares what somebody else thinks, anyway? Every guy just wants to push a pretty girl up against a wall and fuck her. It was just the way things were, but you didn't do it. And now you weren't supposed to say it—or even think it. Big breakthrough.

After the hostess had been called away, the director looked down at the book again. It was funny that people were still writing books. They seemed quaint and vaguely archaic, like an Atari game or an 8-track player. The director knew this was a patronizing sentiment, that he was not supposed to be thinking it, just as he wasn't supposed to think about throwing the airline hostess against the wall and fucking her from behind. But it was true—books didn't make a lot of sense anymore. There was no time for them, they were slow and circumspect. Eventually, of course, there would be no books—just movies, TV series, cable programs, video games. Movies had won. Apparently the message hadn't reached some people.

Without quite knowing why, his mind wandered back to the little tea room in Devon he'd visited a couple of days earlier. He thought of the little tables with the white embroided tablecloths with tea stains. The menus had been designed to look like theater programs. It had been just him and his production assistant and the driver, and no one had recognized him, the great American director. In London, wherever he went, people had whispered and pointed while pretending not to notice him. There'd been a gala event at the National Film Theatre, some sort of lifetime achievement award, television interviews, a party with famous writers and film personalities. But at the tea room in the country he'd felt like he was in another world. There were bookshelves stuffed with old volumes with peeling spines and paperbacks faded from the sun. He'd noticed that other customers, sitting alone, would take a book off a shelf and read it while drinking their tea. The director wondered if this was some sort of old English custom, where tea rooms had merged with municipal libraries to create bastions of cultural sustenance. He couldn't help wondering if it'd all been a show produced secretly for his benefit—a sort of quiet opéra bouffe staged by the British Literacy Council or English Association of Tea Rooms.

The air in the plane had become warm and dry. He put on his headphones connected to his CD player and listened to the jazz he liked so much—Stan Getz and Oscar Peterson.

But still, there was the book.

When he finally opened it, he was relieved to find it was just a collection of stories. He could read one and get a complete narrative in just a few pages. He probably wouldn't like it, but he could tell his assistant that he had tried. He'd gotten a taste of it. It just wasn't his thing. Then he could switch back to the magazines and the screenplay coverage.

He began reading the first story. He wasn't used to so many words filling up a page. A script was a spare, elegant document. A blueprint of exact dimensions. Books were messy, cluttered things.

But this was intriguing. It was written in a lean economical style. It got to the point of things.

The story was about a mother who ordered a cake for her son's birthday. But the boy gets hit by a car on his way to school and he's hospitalized, barely clinging to life. Nobody goes to pick up the cake, so the baker angrily calls the boy's home, disturbing the parents who are consumed by grief.

The director found the story very moving. He could picture it. It had a surprising ending. It was emotional stuff.

He read the other stories and found each one just as gripping as the first. It'd been a long time since he'd been so affected by a writer's words. The simplicity of the language disarmed him.

Had there been a greater purpose to his personal assistant giving him this book? There were signs everywhere, every day, and it was important to sort them out and make the connections, to discover the structure in otherwise random events. The tea room with the books was act one. The handing of the stories to the director was the first turning point. The reading of the stories was act two.

What was the second turning point?

By the time the plane had landed at LAX, the director had not only finished the book, he also had a new mission. People needed to know about this book. He would bring these stories to the public. He would deliver this work to a huge audience, who would share his delight.

He would make the book into a movie.

Of course, there would have to be a few changes. The title would have to go. It was too poetic, too ethereal. The director would have to link the stories together, to solidify the narrative. It'd be a tough squeeze, but he knew people who could do it. It needed to be done fast, and he'd call five or six writers he knew—top people—and each would take a crack at it. The dialogue had to be punched up a bit. Not too much, but enough to make the material move, to make it breathe. The characters were mostly working-class people in the Northwest. He'd bring out the majesty of these working-class people by casting great actors, moving the locale to Los Angeles, and putting in a jazz soundtrack. There would be many roles, but he was famous for his ensemble films. There were a lot of actors—movie stars—who had wanted to work with him. He'd get Julia Roberts and George Clooney. Brad Pitt. Tom Cruise. Cameron Diaz. Everyone would want to work with material like this. It was Salt of the Earth. It was American.

Of course, there were the rights. Maybe the property was already in development. He'd better work fast, in secret. He hoped no one else knew about the book.

As soon as he got off the plane, he took out his cell phone and called his producer. He told him about the book and what he wanted to do. The producer heard the excitement in the director's voice. He sensed that this was the real thing. He'd find out about the rights and call the director right back.

The director was in a limo being driven to his house when the producer called him back ten minutes later. He had some good news, he said: the movie rights were available and the author was dead. They both laughed at this, at the joke of it—but still, it would be helpful. The author wouldn't be around to object to any changes and get in the way of the marketing.

The director instructed the producer to secure the rights and put the English project on hold. We have a movie, he said, and they both, the director and the producer, liked the sound of that. This was going to be a great project. It was Oscar caliber. A classic. This was the reason they were both in the business.

The director looked out at the blur of the streets, at the manicured lawns of the large estates as the limo climbed up the serpentine streets of Beverly Hills. He looked down at the book on his lap with the satisfaction that he would soon own it. He patted the cover affectionately and slipped it back in his Jon Peters bag. Suddenly he felt a sharp ache in his right index finger and looked down to see a sliver of crimson. It was a paper cut, barely an inch long. It was strange how such a small thing could hurt like that—a pulsating, throbbing pain. He stuck the finger in his mouth and sucked the blood clean. He'd couldn't remember ever getting a paper cut from a book before. The thought made him smile. In Hollywood, it was all good, because everything could be regenerated. He would use it. He would put it in the film.

P. G. WODEHOUSE

SHE'S A RIGHT HO, JEEVES

I was still trying to recover from a recent two-day visit from my aunt Livia down from Worcester, who rather liked getting into the sauce. She was a large-breasted woman who had some of the Viking in her (several Vikings, in fact; whenever the Minnesota ice hockey team was in London for a demonstration match). Anyway, she had just left, and despite the seam in my *Times,* the morning had gotten off to a reasonable start. Jeeves had prepared a cracking breakfast, and I was happily reading about the luge finals in St. Moritz—when I heard a crash in the hallway.

"What's that?"

"Just the cat, sir."

I let it go, despite the fact that I didn't have a cat. And it served only to bring the matter of the crease to the fore.

"I say, Jeeves . . . the iron not working this morning?"

"Excuse me, sir?"

"The paper. It has a *crease.*"

"Oh, yes, sir. I do apologise. But things have been a bit . . ." And here he actually trailed off, as if hearing the call of the wild—if Chipping Norton could be said to have a wild. Just then I noticed an odd-looking young man, definitely the wrong side of twenty-one, skulking about the hall. I asked Jeeves about it.

"Oh, that would be my nephew, sir—Peeves."

"Well what's he doing here?"

"I'm grooming him to take my place, should anything untoward happen to me, sir."

"Are you expecting anything untoward, Jeeves?"

"No, sir. It's merely a precautionary measure. He is my gentleman's gentleman."

"You can't be serious."

"I am, sir. But I've instructed him to assist you in any way he can. He knows that he might be my gentleman's gentleman, but he's *your* gentleman's gentleman's gentleman."

"*Is* he a gentleman?"

"Well, we shall have to see, sir, shan't we?"

I returned to reading about the luge finals and had a bite of toast. Jeeves has perfected the art of toasting by applying a light layer of prebuttering, toasting it, and then adding a brush-up butter coat. Delectable. And then Jeeves insisted on puncturing my pleasantly inflated mood.

"If you don't mind me saying so, sir, you're looking a bit . . . insubstantial this morning."

"Insub *what*?"

"Stantial. Your Boiler Room membership card is getting a tad dusty."

"Dash it, Jeeves, say what you mean. Are you inferring that I'm not hitting the gym enough? Is that it?"

"It is just a suggestion, sir."

"I never should have joined that infernal place in the first place. In the second place, I hardly ever get down to London in the third place. And in the fourth place, I don't think that it's any of your business in the first place!"

"Very good, sir."

He collected the breakfast things and placed them on a tray.

"Shall I put out your swimming paraphernalia, sir?"

"Why?"

"Did you not agree to go swimming with Julia Gogglesworth this afternoon?"

"No, no, that's weeks away. March fourth."

"Which is today, sir."

"But that's . . . No, no, I think you've that wrong because . . ." I picked up the morning's *Times*. He was right. It was March fourth. "Oh no. She mustn't see me in this state. I can't go swimming. My arms look like . . . like . . ."

"Chopsticks?"

"Thank you, Jeeves. Chopsticks, exactly."

"Might I make a suggestion, sir?"

"If it involves going to the gym—"

"No, sir. But my nephew Peeves is roughly your hue and height. He could pose as you at the swimming baths. He looks very healthy in his swimming trunks."

"Is that right?"

"Yes, sir. He was an alternate on the Malta Olympic swim team."

"Malta, eh?"

"Yes, sir."

"Is he not English then?"

"He is English. But he's a mercenary. And he got accepted as an alternate."

"Alternate what?"

"Swimmer, sir."

"Was he an actual alternate, or was he an alternate's alternate? Or was he an alternate's alternate's alternate?"

Jeeves neglected to laugh. "He was an alternate, sir."

Rarely gets my jokes, that Jeeves.

I have never really understood the need for athletic encounters. Shooting is about the limit for my exertions—and if truth be told, it's really the birds who get most of the exercise. We just like to blow them out of the sky from a standing position. And since I brought a couple of golf carts over from Texas, there hasn't been much walking during shooting either.

And so I can't remember what compelled me to accept Julia's invitation to a swimming party at the Chelsea Baths. At the time the event seemed so far off I assumed I would have bulked up enough by the time to present an inviting figure. We Woosters are built like stick insects, an unfortunate physique compounded by eight hundred

years of relative indolence. It is said that my great ancestor Ebenezer
Wooster was the first Briton to be killed at Agincourt when the
weight of his armour pulled him off his horse before the trumpet
was even sounded. He was evidently trampled underfoot by Henry V
himself. This accounts for the trampled figure on the lower left of
the family's coat of arms. The upper-right figure is a silhouette representing Crusty Wooster falling off the HMS *Victory* en route to
Trafalgar. Apparently he was addressed by Admiral Nelson, which so
intimidated him that he stepped back and slipped off the ship. Again,
it was the first casualty of a major British campaign. Woosters have
also inaugurated fatalities at Blenheim, Waterloo, the Crimea, and the
Marne. Thus the family's motto: *Mortes Primus non Disgustum* (To die
first is no disgrace).

Peeves drove me to London in the Morgan two-seater. He was not
a very talkative fellow.

"So, you're Jeeves's nephew, is that right?"

"If that's what he told you, sir."

"You aren't, then?"

"I aren't what, sir?"

"Oh, skip it."

"Yes, sir."

The ensuing silence only unnerved me, so I launched another
stab at conversation.

"I understand you were a Malteser."

"Sir?"

"On the alternate Olympic swim team."

"Oh, I see, yes. The correct term for a person of Maltese extrac-
tion is Maltesan, which I actually am not, having been born in
Oxfordshire. Unless you were making a pun on the popular English chocolate delicacy, in which case: very amusing."

We drove on in silence for a while. I was a tad steamed. Finally I
said, "Rather kills the joke, really."

"Yes, sir."

I have to admit, he was built like a Grenadier Guard—a species
Julia had been coincidentally drawn to in the past. But I didn't see

the facial resemblance between us at all, and I didn't understand how we could get away with posing as one person.

"Oh no."

"What is it, sir?"

"What colour are your shorts?"

"Excuse me, sir?"

"Your swimming shorts. What colour are they?"

"Blue, sir."

"Blast. Mine are red. We won't match."

"I took the precaution of bringing an extra pair of trunks in my colour, sir."

"Oh good. Thanks. I suppose you might be Jeeves's nephew after all."

"Yes, sir."

When we reached the Chelsea Baths, Julia was waiting for me outside the entrance. She was wearing a sleeveless white dress and looked smashing, despite her granny specs.

"I say, Bertie, I'm glad you could make it. Where's Jeeves?"

"Oh, he has the day off. I drove myself down."

"Really? I didn't think you were driving since that smash-up you had on Whitehall."

She was referring to a minor scrape I'd had a few months earlier when my Packard touring car leapt up on the pavement and chipped a bit of knee off the statue of Sir Francis Drake outside the Admiralty. My friends supportively claimed to prefer Drake in this post-mishap state. Pickles Dupree said he looked "far more dangerous and chic." But it rather put me off getting behind the wheel again.

"Oh no, I'm back in the driver's seat, ha ha."

"Well I hope you've been practicing your swimming, because I'm going to race you within an inch of your life."

I didn't doubt it. When Julia had gone inside I motioned to Peeves, who was hiding across the street behind a lamppost. He trotted over to me, carrying his small duffel bag and handing me a small blue ball of fabric.

"What's this?"

"Your swimming trunks, sir."

In the changing room we worked out a series of coded whistles to orchestrate our double act. We had the small advantage that, without her glasses, Julia was blind as the proverbial bat, and hopefully Peeves and I could switch places in a quick blur, and Julia would be none the wiser.

There was, however, the unfortunate situation of Peeves's shorts—specifically, the size of his bulkhead. Simply stated, our naughty nether regions were not quite on an equal footing, nor were our waists of the same magnitude. Thus I was put in the position of having to hold up the bathing costume with one hand, while carrying on my normal business (swimming, waving, gesticulating) with the other. Though not a naturally demonstrative man with my hands, I was nonetheless at a 50 percent disadvantage especially in the pool where I did not normally excel even in the most favourable of circumstances. The plan, of course, was that Peeves would play me, so to speak, in the action shots (especially diving) and mid shots (displaying his muscular torso). I would play myself in the extreme close-ups (wearing a towel) and all dialogue scenes. (You will notice a certain familiarity with cinematic language, acquired from several years of studying *Screen Gems* and the *Motion Picture Almanac*.) Hopefully our "special effects" would not be marred by two "Woosters" in the same frame, and for a while this ruse worked surprisingly well; as Julia watched foggily from across the pool, I called out and waved to her, then waited for her focus to be sidetracked (luckily, a child squealed with exceptional timing, diverting her attention) and I whistled for Peeves to perform stunt double duty. As Julia turned our way, he dove spectacularly in and effected a swim stroke of charismatic agility. Julia was riveted as he climbed up out of the pool before her in a slow, powerful gesture that generously displayed "my" impressive arms and abdominal muscles. (I couldn't help noticing Julia's approving reaction, as she clapped her hands in a tap-tap involuntary applause.) I tooted the whistle signalling a change of performers—and as Julia searched the pool for the source of the sound, I seized the moment to grab a towel and appear in front of her. "Hey-ho."

"I say, Bertie, you *have* been working out, haven't you?"

"Oh, just a few hours a day. You know—when I can."

She reached out to sample a towel-covered pectoral, but I darted out of her grasp.

"Are you dry already?"

"Oh—yes, I drip-dry with surprising alacrity. Care for a race?"

A sly smile sneaked into her lips. "Okay. But what do I get if I win?"

"If you win . . ." I had to think quickly, in the presumptuous mind of Charles Atlas. "Er . . . Then I have to give you a complete rubdown."

Her sly smile had gotten bigger. "And if *you* win?"

"Then you have to give *me* a rubdown."

"Ooh. One-two-three-go!" Suddenly she dove into the pool and I was still standing in my towel, holding up my trunks. Without thinking, I dove in after her.

I interrupt this narrative for a brief historical anecdote. We Woosters are not famous for the curve of our derrieres—quite the contrary, we tend to possess behinds of almost mathematical flatness. My great-uncle Favius Wooster, in fact, survived his brother in the Battle of Neuve Chapelle only to be taken prisoner by the Germans and used as an ironing board. (He returned home in 1918, five inches thinner but two inches taller, and became famous for having "the greatest posture in England.") My own backside has the usual Woosterian Bauhaus effect, and so, as I pierced the skin of the water, in that terrible whoosh I could feel the blue trunks shoot off me.

As I came up for air I could hear several swimmers laughing, including some beastly children who insisted on pointing out, to the few people who had missed it, the glorious event before them. Julia was still racing, oblivious to my unfortunate mishap and the rambunctious mirth it had produced. I looked back at Peeves who, watching from the entrance to the men's changing room, quickly assessed the situation and dove in—I assumed to retrieve my shorts. Instead he coursed through the water, slick as a seal, past me and up the full length of the pool. He touched the far end at the same moment that Julia reached it—a photo finish. They turned to each other and laughed, and Peeves helped her out of the pool.

What happened then is murky to me; I was faced with the choice of watching the Julia drama unfold or diving down to scoop up my shorts. Needless to say, I chose the more modest option. When I returned to the surface, gripping the trunks for dear life, both Peeves and Julia were gone.

Two weeks later I was sitting in bed when Jeeves brought in my breakfast tray with the morning's *Times.*

"You'll be proud of me, Jeeves. I'm going to drive down to London today and give that gym such a smacking, you won't recognize me."

"Today, sir?" said Jeeves skeptically.

"Why, what's wrong with today?"

"I regret to remind you that your aunt Livia is arriving today."

"But dash it, Jeeves, she was just here!"

"Yes, but I understand the Minnesota Vikings are appearing in London for a Royal Command Performance at the Palladium."

"Oh well. Better lock up the cocktails."

"Yes, sir," said Jeeves dourly.

I looked up and noticed he was effecting one of his melancholy, missing-the-bayou countenances.

"What's wrong, Jeeves?"

"This just arrived, sir." He handed me a card displaying a tinted picture of a palm tree on a beach. I turned it over. It was a *carte postale* from Julia on the Côte d'Azur. "Having a smashing time with your cousin Peeves. Would you be an angel and post him his shorts? The ones he had quickly got torn to shreds and he can't find anything in his size." I couldn't help noticing that she had underlined "size" three times.

"That Julia is a right ho, Jeeves," I said.

"Indeed, sir."

"Now she thinks Peeves is *my* cousin. What an insult. He'd never make an ironing board."

"Excuse me, sir?"

"And he's certainly no gentleman."

"Or gentleman's gentleman," added Jeeves.

"Quite right. Speaking of ironing boards, super work on the *Times,* Jeeves. No crease at all. They really ought to print them this way."

"Yes, sir. I'll drop them a note."

J. D. SALINGER

LATER WORK

Britney Spears
Jive Records
BMG
New York, NY

Dear Britney,

I can see from your video that you are not a girl, but not yet a woman. I understand this phenomenon, having written about it extensively. You may know my work. I am the author of "Franny," which really could be called "Oops, I Did It Again!" (that was, in fact, its original title). Franny was from a large family, a kind of urban, intellectual, Jewish-Irish "Mickey Mouse Club," and had trouble getting attention, which is why she chose to go on tour, dancing and lip-synching to sexually knowing songs. (This part was edited out of the final draft, but astute readers have always understood this subtext.)

If you would like to finally become a woman, I'd be happy to have you as a guest at my New Hampshire hideaway, which is nestled in a comfy compound surrounded by an electric fence with razor wire. I know how exhausting being in the public eye can be, and if you choose to stay with me, I can promise no one would find you for months.

> Yours,
> Jerry Salinger
> (Not Jerry Seinfeld. Some people get us confused.)

Terry Gross
National Public Radio
Washington, DC

Dear Terry,

Many mornings I wake up to your sweet voice on my radio, interviewing those lousy morons who are strictly from hunger. They don't deserve you, Terry—that rude Gene Simmons ought to get whacked.

I know when you talk to your guests you are thinking: "Why don't they understand me? Why don't they see me for who I am?" I can't see you, Terry, and yet I know who you are: a young, precocious woman who has always been smarter than everyone around you, who is taken for granted but not recognized as the burgeoning sexual being that you are. From your voice I'd guess that you're just out of college and probably on your way to grad school.

Why don't you take some time off? You should come up here for some *real* "fresh air."

> Cheers,
> Jerry "J.D." Salinger

Zoë
c/o Ritz Modeling Agency
114 Lafayette St.
New York, NY

Dear Zoë,

I couldn't believe my eyes when I saw you in that Bebe ad in last month's *Jane* magazine. You look just like Phoebe from *The Catcher in the Rye*. I assumed your smudged eye shadow and lipstick were on purpose, as well as that torn, rain-soaked silk blouse. That really killed me. Or had you just been ravished by an unscrupulous photographer who threatened to blackball you in the business if you dared complain to your agency? Anyway, I hope you're feeling better.

You certainly look like someone who could use some taking care of. Let me be that someone. I have a lot of land with a pond with a lot of ducks. I can never figure out where all the ducks go when the pond freezes over. Do you think a guy comes round and collects them all in a sack?

So anyway, why don't you drive up to visit me? If you're too young to drive, I could have a car pick you up in New York.

> Ciao,
> Jerry Salinger

Katie Holmes
WB Network
Burbank, CA

Dear Katie,

What are you doing with that dweeb Dawson? He clearly lacks a certain testicularity that is the hallmark of the section man. (That Dawson creaks!) You should blow that college. It blows. I was thrown out of five schools and never went to college. It's strictly for the birds.

Anyway, your womanly form throbs in those little-girl costumes they put you in. I can see you are bursting to get out.

So get out—come up to Cornish, NH. I'm currently developing "Franny" as a film property, and I think you might be just right for the role. (And what do you think of Tobey Maguire for Zooey, with Ang Lee to direct?) Let's talk!

> Peace out,
> J. D. Salinger

Winona Ryder
c/o Creative Artists Management
Beverly Hills, CA

Dear Winona,

I understand exactly what happened in Saks Fifth Avenue. Boo-Boo had a kleptomania problem too. You're obviously going through a lot of stress. Your latest film choices have been less than spectacular, and Angelina Jolie hijacked your own movie. (Girl interrupted indeed!)

Listen: We're tapping Johnny Depp (Episcopalean?) or Joaquin Phoenix (Catholic?) for Zooey. But the part of Franny really needs an assimilated Jew like you to pull it off. With your big saucer eyes, lost stare, and boxy sweaters hiding your ample form, you positively *reek* of troubled coed. But I think you should come up to New Hampshire so we can talk about it.

Yours,
Jerry Salinger

Jennifer Love Hewitt
Love Productions
Warner Bros.
Burbank, CA

Dear Love,

You *are* Audrey Hepburn. And you are Franny too. I heard you were interested in the role but were told that I refused to give up the film rights. That's only partly true—I've been holding on to them until I found my Franny. (By the way, I actually met Audrey Hepburn a few times. Contrary to popular opinion, she *hated* children and animals, and I actually saw her once—furious at some particularly phlegmatic room service—throw a calico cat out of her eighth-floor window at the Ritz Hotel in Paris. I think it *just* missed the obelisk, but landed on a Deux Chevaux.) Anyway, your sleek form with that mammarial overbite fits to a T (and what T's!) my bodacious conception of Franny Glass. We're in discussions with Sean Penn or Josh Hartnett for Zooey.

I read in *Seventeen* that you're crazy about your diet. Don't worry—I'm completely macrobiotic. So jump in an industry jet and get your sweet self up here. The closest airport is at Concord, where I can pick you up in my Lincoln Navigator.

Sincerely,
J. D. Salinger

Chelsea Clinton
Stanford University
Stanford, CA

To Chelsea (with Love and Squalor),

I always got a bang out of your dad. I think he was a real prince of a guy. I'm not kidding. And he read books too, as I'm sure you do. Hey, remember Phoebe in *Catcher in the Rye*? You remind me of her. If I had a record of "Little Shirley Beans," I'd send it to you. I've watched you grow up, from a gangly duckling to a beautiful, charming swan with a clear intellectual advantage. I could use a young mind with a fresh view to help me edit my 6,192-page "Glass Family saga." I think the project will probably take several months, so it makes sense that you move up here. Any Secret Service agents you need could stay in the barn.

Diplomatically yours,
Jerome David Salinger

Kate Beckinsdale
c/o Dreamworks
Los Angeles, CA

Dear Kate,

I didn't think *Pearl Harbor* was *that* bad (well, no worse than the real attack). I was at D day and believe me, if you'd been in World War Two, we could have wrapped up the whole shebang by the end of 1944!

Seriously, though, you're not burdened with that self-conscious moronic stab at an accent. Every time Julianne Moore tries to sound English, she looks like she's about to swallow her goddam tongue. She speaks like an epileptic, as if she's gonna have a lousy breakdown about every five minutes.

Anyway, have you ever given any thought to playing Franny of *Franny and Zooey*? I always saw her as slightly English myself, but producers have been pushing Jennifer Love Hewitt on me. Can you imagine? Strictly from hunger. For Zooey, we're thinking Jeremy Northam or Jude Law, with Oliver Stone to direct.

Anyway, do drop me a line, stating point of view. Yours sincerely, wasting away.

Right ho,
Jerome Salinger

Jennifer Lopez
Epic Records
Times Square
New York, NY

Dear J.Lo,

¿Cómo es tú? Caught U on the American Applause Awards on the E! channel. Great set! (And congrats on the three Amapps!) You sure can shake yo' booty!

Thought U were great in that film with whatsisname.

U've probably heard about the Hollywood stampede for the part of F in the upcoming Baz Luhrman project *Salinger's F & Z.* For Z we're talking about Leonardo or maybe Russell Crowe (if we can get him to shave or shed a few pounds). But for F we really need a sexy Latina to get it on.

Why don't you come up to NH so we can discuss it. I have a full set of weights, so you can workout while you're here.

Word up, yo,
Jay-D. Sal

RONALD REAGAN

ITCH: A MEMOIR OF EDMUND MORRIS

I'll never forget the first time I saw Edmund Morris—or "Itch" as everyone called him. It was 1927 and I was working as a lifeguard on the Rock River. Reading my Edgar Rice Burroughs, I looked up and saw a young, bearded, flaxen-haired youth staring at me, admiring my physique. He was jotting down notes on a little pad, and when he realized he'd been caught out, he darted back behind a tree. Then, suddenly, fleet-footed, he ran out to the river and began swimming to the middle, where he proceeded to begin drowning. I swam out and saved him. This happened again the next day—the same bearded youth, the same notepad, the same odd dash to the middle of the river. I saved Itch seventy-seven times that summer and he never once thanked me. And each time, after I'd pulled him ashore and breathed life back into his fragile lungs, he'd introduce himself as if we'd never met before.

But that's the way it was with Itch. He lived his whole life as if he were the subject of a major biography. At times he was quick-witted with an easy laugh, fully engaged in conversation, speaking in a clipped English accent. But other times he seemed removed, distant, an apparent airhead, inventing stories of his past out of thin air. He talked incessantly of his son, telling anecdote after anecdote about little Gavin leading antiwar demonstrations at Berkeley, blowing up chemistry labs, levitating the Pentagon. It was only later that I learned that this "son" didn't exist at all.

INT. WHITE HOUSE—DAY

Dutch and Itch are sitting in the Oval Office. Itch is wearing a gray gabardine suit. Dutch is the president of the United States.

ITCH: Remember when he walked through the golden arch of the Paramount lot, the sun glazing off the edges like Osiris in a thousand little fires? This was America in the very bosom of its innocence, creating the bubble that defined it for generations, the dream factory in which every man, woman, and child lived in the promised land.
DUTCH: Actually, I worked at Warners.

His ignorance was encyclopedic. He had no sense of political history or economic theory, but he could spend hours waxing nostalgic about his old school days in England. If you asked him about East–West relations, he'd immediately launch into a half-baked story about how some of the top stars in Hollywood had been kept out of the Communist Party for being "flaky."

Also, Itch could go on and on about his days working on the Warner lot, hanging out at the commissary, and coaching me on my roles in *Dark Victory* and *Kings Row.* It seemed odd that I couldn't remember him in Hollywood, and odder still when I calculated that he could only have been a year old when these films were made.

Then in 1992 came the defining moment of Itch's life. While walking on the Eureka College campus, he stepped on an acorn and had a nervous breakdown.

INT. BIOGRAPHER'S CONVENTION—DAY

Itch lurches unsteadily toward the podium. Is he drunk? He reaches the dais and grasps the sides with both hands.

ITCH: Friends . . . I am a lost man. I've been paid three million dollars to write a biography about an empty man, an idiot really, who became the governor of California, the president of the United States, and the Savior of the Free World. But where's the story?

I went to visit him in the hospital. He looked tired and drained, and claimed he'd lost almost half his blood. But when he saw me he smiled, and when he cracked a joke—"I hope none of the doctors here are biographers"—I knew he was on the road to recovery.

INT. SAGMORE HILL—DAY

Teddy Roosevelt is showing Reagan his prized collection of trophies, the animal heads sticking out from the walls like hairy gargoyles.

DUTCH: Great heads.
TEDDY: Hah!
DUTCH: Terrific house.
TEDDY: Ha-hah! Bully-bully!
DUTCH: Teddy, I wanted to ask you—what was it like to work with Edmund Morris? He wrote a book about you. Was he always trying to insert himself into the narrative?
TEDDY: Not at all! Itch was a complete gentleman. But sometimes he did seem like an apparent airhead. He'd go on about his friend Paul Rae, reading me letters and newspaper articles his friend had supposedly written. But later I found that this friend did not exist! It was very odd, what? Bully-bully!

When Itch started to lose his mind he wrote a very touching letter to the American people. In part it read: "Dear America, I'm losing my mind." It's difficult for me to read those words without thinking about the great book he could have written about me if he hadn't gone crazy. Someday, I hope, he will recover his senses and write the biography we've all been waiting for. Until then, I'll be waiting by the pool, raking the leaves.

LILLIAN HELLMAN

IMPLAUSIMENTO

I would not have felt the need to tell the story of my "Nuremberg Adventure" had it not been so misrepresented by others. Years after the fact, certain episodes of one's past often take on a life of their own. But in setting down this account, I have adhered as strictly to the facts as possible.

It happened that in June 1936 I was in London to attend the British premiere of my play called *The Children's Hour*. A playwright can often feel like the most superfluous person at her own production, and such was the case in the days leading up to opening night. It was not a bad production, though I questioned their casting John Gielgud in the role of the headmistress. (He turned out to be very good.)

I was not, in fact, looking forward to opening night, a ritual of faux bonhomie and repressed schadenfreude. I was therefore not adverse to seizing an opportunity that would afford me the excuse to skip my own premiere. It came that afternoon when I was handed a letter by a mysterious stranger. It read simply: "Please come to the Savoy Hotel this evening at 7:30 P.M. Room 1312. It is a matter of the utmost emergency. A friend."

I assumed it was Amanda Friend, a horrible girl I knew slightly from New York University. She owed me fifty dollars for an abortion I'd financed some years before. I wondered if she'd actually had the operation or birthed the child and absconded with the money—or if she'd even been pregnant in the first place. (Thinking back on it, I thought it unlikely that any man in his right mind would agree to sleep with her.) I was intrigued, and so that evening I took a cab to the hotel.

The woman who answered the door was not Amanda Friend at all, but Claudine Tessamont, the motley-looking mistress of my former boss at Horace Liveright.

Tessamont was a small woman with red hair, a fat, freckled face, and a big stomach. She asked me if I'd told anyone about the meeting. I said no. Good, she said, and ushered me quickly into the room, where we sat on large armchairs. The drapes were closed.

"Is it true that you're planning to go to Berlin?" she asked.

I answered that I had planned a short trip, but how did she know?

She ignored the question. "We'd like you to take a brief detour to Nuremberg."

"Who is this 'we'?" I asked.

"Please don't ask any questions. But it's very important that you deliver a box of chocolates to Adolf Hitler."

"Why?"

"It would help us. He has a weakness for Cadbury's Black Magic. If you could hand him the chocolates—and then get yourself as far away as fast as possible—I can't tell you how helpful you would be to us. Many people you don't know would be very grateful."

She handed me the package before I'd even had time to think about the assignment. What did I care if Hitler got a box of chocolates? But it has always been my affliction to help unknown people in need.

It was on the train between Paris and Berlin that I first noticed the ticking. Knowing little about foreign chocolate I thought nothing of it. I had heard that some European chocolate had to "settle" and that this might make a slight ticking sound.

I attended the Nuremberg rally, watching with dismay half a million German men march in formation. It was a sickening sight, I must admit, and I got no closer to Hitler than several hundred yards. But then, through some theatrical friends in Berlin, I obtained an invitation to an exclusive party in the Banhofgartenbegotenzinginghasbaden, at which all the high German command were expected. I hoped fervently that Hitler would make an appearance, so I could give him the gift of the chocolates.

Unfortunately, there was no Hitler, and I was beginning to feel a little unwelcome. Did the elegantly dressed swells in their evening clothes know a Jewess was among them? It mattered little to me now if Hitler got his chocolates or not. I was about to leave when a hush fell on the crowd and I saw Herr Hitler arrive with a small retinue of officers. I stepped forward. "Herr Hitler, I would like to present you with this box of Cadbury chocolates from a group of friends in England."

"Ah yes, the lovely Mitford sisters, no doubt," he said in heavily accented but perfect English. His eyes sparkled at the sight of the chocolates, and he reached out for them when another hand grabbed the box.

"Oh, *chocolates!*" said an American woman. I turned around to see it was Mary McCarthy.

"Mary, get your hands off that. What are you doing here?"

"Oh, I *love* Nazis," said Mary. "Aren't they cute?"

By now Hitler had been whisked away and was chatting with other guests. Mary had the lid of the box off and was already dipping into the small delicacies. "Hmm, great! I love these!"

"These were for Mr. Hitler," I protested.

"Oh, he has plenty of chocolate. Besides, he's getting a bit *zaftig* around the *middenhof,* if you know what I mean. Do you hear ticking?"

I grabbed the box from her hands and rushed to the ladies' room, where I flushed it down the toilet.

I was already halfway to the station when I heard the explosion. The damage to the Nuremberg plumbing system, I later learned, was so extensive that subsequent rallies had to be held in Berlin.

Although McCarthy wasn't killed in the blast, she suffered a brain concussion from a falling chandelier that had a pronounced effect on her literary ability. Read in this light, her subsequent work is less dreadful when one considers it was written with a severe mental handicap.

In the late forties, she persuaded her uncle, the despicable Senator Joe McCarthy, to launch an anti-Communist crusade. He trampled on constitutional rights with his series of unconscionable witch hunts. Though asked to testify, I respectfully declined the invitation, stating, "I will not cut my conscience to fit Mary McCarthy's fashions."

Argumento

It was forty years before I was to see Mary McCarthy again, when we were both booked on the same *Dick Cavett Show*. It was an unfortunate meeting. I had just finished giving an account of my Nuremberg adventure, when Mary interrupted me. "That's the most ridiculous story I've ever heard," she said.

"It isn't. You ruined my one chance to assassinate Adolf Hitler. Face it: You're at least partly responsible for World War Two."

"The idea that I 'loved' Nazis . . . I wasn't anywhere *near* Nuremberg in 1936. Do you want to see my passport?"

"You expect me to believe your passport?"

"Everything you say is a lie," she said. "Even 'and,' 'if,' and 'but.' "

"I didn't say 'but.' "

"That's a lie."

Dick Cavett tried to interject. "Ladies . . ."

"And Senator Joe McCarthy wasn't my uncle, you idiot."

"No?" I said. "And I suppose Bunny Wilson wasn't your husband."

"For just a few years. At least he wasn't a ninety-eight-pound weakling who smoked three packs a day."

"Hammett only smoked two packs. Three on the weekend."

"I once saw a seventeen-year-old arthritic Persian cat beat the shit out of him."

"Ladies," said Cavett. "Excuse me, but—"

"Wilson looked like a bulldog. He means nothing today. No one's heard of him. No one's heard of *you*."

"And who are you? Jane Fonda?"

"You're such a Jew."

"You're such a Catholic."

"A *lapsed* Catholic."

"*All* Catholics are lapsed!"

Dick Cavett, who had been trying to get a word in edgewise for some time, stood up, unbuckled his belt, and let his trousers fall to the floor. He was wearing red, white, and blue boxer shorts. There was a sudden hushed silence in the studio.

"Glad I could finally get everyone's attention." He pulled his pants up. "Now, I do think Mary has a point. I don't think I'd be going out on a limb to say that Senator Joe McCarthy was not her uncle."

"Thank you, Dick," said Mary.

"As for being responsible for not killing Hitler, I'd have to admit that I wasn't there at the time, so I have no idea what happened in Nuremberg in 1936."

"I appreciate it," I said.

"But the reason I brought the two of you on today was not, in fact, to bicker, but to discuss my new book *Cavett Caveat*. I was hoping to get a couple of blurbs."

"Here's a blurb," I said. "Mary McCarthy is a whore of the first order."

She got up to slap me, but I surprised her with a left hook and sent her sailing to the mat.

Two weeks later I got a call that I'd won the Nobel Prize, and that Mary McCarthy was suing me for 3.5 million dollars. The resulting controversy scared the Swedes enough to postpone the Nobel, and I countersued Mary for 4.5 million. She then founded the Symbionese Liberation Army that kidnapped Patty Hearst. She died a couple of years later in flagrante delicto with Nelson Rockefeller.

BRIDGET JONES

THE DIARY OF ANAÏS NIN

January 12

Cigarettes 3 (not bad), Pernods 2 (little ones), poems 3 (v. good)

Ugh. Another cable from Daddy saying he wants to sleep with me. Not a good start for the year. Also, have inaugurated a flirtation with Henry Miller, who seems to thrive on flattery, but is so difficult to read! Received a letter from him this morning:

> Dear Anaïs,
> Saw you on the Blvd. Montparnasse yesterday afternoon. Your dress really is too revealing.
> What are you up to?
>
> Yours,
Henry

I immediately wrote back:

Dear Henry,
Not sure what the dress is up to, but I'm strictly up to no good.
Do I deserve a spanking?

> Yours,
> Anaïs

Two hours later I received this note by *pneu:*

Dear Anaïs,
Spanking? It's your husband who's English, not me. What you
need is a good fucking, and if I fuck you, you'll stay fucked. Your
cunt will be spitting out gold coins.

> Yours,
> Henry

Thought that was a bit cheeky. But I decided to play along. Sent
him the following note:

Dear H,
Are you implying I'm some sort of slot machine?
Sorry to disappoint. I'm just a woman. With a revealing dress.

> Yours,
> A

Ran down to the post office in Louveciennes to pop it off. Waited
several hours, but no reply. Oh, why does Paris have such a dreadful postal system—only five deliveries a day, and Henry must have
just missed the last one. Or did he not even bother to respond? I
know I'll never get to sleep tonight.

January 14

Cigarettes 2 (good), croissants 3 (bad), poems negative 3 (see below)

Date with Henry in his room at the L'Hôtel Cafard. We made
love for six hours while reading each other's work and talking
about Lawrence and Rilke and Strindberg. By the third hour,
paper was getting stuck to my bottom and I noticed that some of

the ink was blurring. Lost three poems and half a diary. Then we fell asleep in each other's arms but were soon woken up by the bedbugs. Why am I so attracted to bohemians? I have a perfectly decent bourgeois husband. A car. A sweet little house in the *banlieue*. Hugo loves me, and yet there is no passion. And he never writes me letters. Received three from Henry yesterday before lunch. His wife is coming in next week from New York—the mysterious Gypsy June Smith. (Or is she a Jewess? Henry is coy about that. But "Smith"—not a very Jewish name.) Henry says he isn't sure if he's still in love with her, and in any case she doesn't have my literary prowess. What I want to know is what she does have. Henry said he's resigned to sleeping with her for at least as long as she's here. It's all he's been talking about for days.

Are my breasts big enough? Are my eyes too large?

February 7

Pernods 2 (large ones—v. bad), cigarettes 3 (hmm . . .), poems O (bad), absinthe 1 (what was I thinking?)

Ugh! Letter from Henry: "I must see you." Took a taxi to Clichy intending to sleep with him. When I got there, Fred said Henry had just gone to Louveciennes to sleep with me. Slept with Fred. Took the bus back.

Got home to find Hugo in an odd, exhausted state. He said he'd had a particularly athletic workout in the garden.

"Oh yes?" I said. "Who attacked you?"

"It was the weeds, actually. They practically *strangled* the African violets."

The swashbuckling life of my dear old English husband—gardening in February.

"Oh, you just missed Henry," he said, rubbing his gloves on his trousers.

"Oh yes?" I said, feigning disinterest.

"Yes, he just left on his bicycle. Funny chap, that."

"Henry? In what way?"

"Golly, I don't know. He always seems to have so much *energy*."

Little does he know . . .

February 13

Chocolate 8 grams (oh dear), cigarettes 6 (and Gitanes!), poems 1 (and not v. good)

Funny how Henry *looks* like a monk, but Hugo *is* like a monk.

I could kill for some escargots.

June is indeed beautiful—in that Gypsy-dance-hall way. She has the biggest boobs! No wonder Henry likes her. What do her nipples look like? She has no eyebrows—she just pencils them in. Does Henry like that? I've always taken him for an armpit hair and eyebrows man.

Oh, why doesn't he answer my letters? Perhaps he *is* sleeping with his wife. Does he find me too bourgeois? Are my breasts too small? Are my eyebrows thin enough? Is my bottom too big? Maybe I shouldn't have called his book "Tropic of Canker." But it was a joke!

March 4

Cigarettes 12 (Galoises—bad), Pernods 6 (v. bad), poems 0 (despicable)

No word from Henry. Had to sleep with Wambly Bald, and then ran into Fred at Le Dome, so decided to sleep with him. Then when I got home, Hugo was in the garden again, sweating in his business suit and pulling out the hydrangeas.

"Oh, you just missed Henry," he said.

"Oh yes?" I said, with superbly forged boredom. "What did he want?"

"He said he missed you. I thought that was very sweet."

"Yes, he . . . can be sweet."

"Look at what a mess the squirrels made of my garden," he said, pointing at a pile of dirt. And then, "What happened to your stockings?"

I looked down at my legs. I wasn't wearing my stockings—must have left them at Fred's. "Oh, they got laddered, so I took them off."

"You poor dear," he said, heading into the house.

I couldn't be sure, but his footwear looked different. "Are you wearing Henry's shoes?" I said.

"Oh—yes. His were falling apart, so I gave him mine. I'm using these for gardening."

My sweet, kind, poor fool of a husband—giving his wife's lover the shoes off his own feet!

March 15

Cigarettes 8 (but Marlboros), whiskeys 5 (see below), pain au chocolat 4 (terrible)

Aargh. Will never drink again. Had dinner with June at La Rotunde. She's a real brassy American with hot red lips and a bombshell figure. She kept telling me how beautiful I was, "like a goddamn Botticelli." And can she drink! Had five whiskeys, and I was still three behind her. She invited me back to her hotel room so she could read me some of her poems. When we got there, I said, "Where's Henry?"

"Oh, he's off some doing some goddamn research."

I was feeling a little light-headed, so June put me in her bed and started kissing my forehead—which did make me feel a bit better. Then she got in the bed with me.

Gosh, June certainly knows what she wants (and gets it). We made love for seven hours while reading each other's poems and discussing Sappho, Dostoyevsky, and Marlene Dietrich. Then I fell asleep.

Woke up and screamed—there was an evil dwarf staring at me from the foot of the bed!

"What is it?" said June

I pointed at the dwarf.

"Oh, that's just Monsieur Fang, my devil doll. He goes every-where with me."

I'd heard Henry mention Monsieur Fang, but I always thought it was just a joke. June went over and kissed Monsieur Fang on his face. It was a long kiss, and as she whispered sweet nothings to him, I couldn't help noticing she was also feeling him up. A curious woman.

Got home shortly after midnight to find Hugo in the garden, planting seeds in the dark. He was wearing his pajamas.

"Hugo? What are you doing out here?"

"Oh, you just missed Henry."

"Hmm?"

"Interesting chap. Left a book for you." He looked absently around the garden.

I was too tired to ask about it, and went up to bed. Was surprised to find Henry's socks in the bed, and asked Hugo about it.

"Oh, uh. Yes, he needed a new pair of socks, so I gave him mine."

"But why are his in the bed?"

"Ah, yes . . . I was trying to press them."

April 14

Pâté 16 grams (a lot), brie 18 grams (but I didn't eat all of it—well, most of it), baguettes 2 (very embarrassing)

Letter from Henry, explaining everything:

Dear A,

Heard you found my socks in your bed. Thought you knew: it's an old Zen custom to bestow good luck on the occupant. By the way, June said she had a great time with you. As did Fred. Hope to see you soon.

Love,
H

So he knows! But at least he explained the sock thing. Received another letter from Daddy begging me to go to Mexico and become his love slave. Why does everyone want to sleep with me? (And why do I want to sleep with everyone?) Sent Daddy a cable saying I had my hands rather full at the moment, but I'd think about it.

EDWARD ALBEE

ANNOYING PLAY W/ DOG

General Comments/Note on Staging

For this play to work according to its intentions, careful attention must be paid to the stage directions and to the play's form and counterpoint. The twenty-foot "invisible" dog is completely real to the people on stage, and should be depicted either by a huge hologram or a photograph projected on a screen. The French-speaking armless dwarf must be played by a real dwarf (preferably one who speaks French; arms are optional). If he can't sing "La Marseillaise" completely believably, then the whole conceit of the play collapses. Also, it is imperative that the Annoying Old Lady be seen not to annoy but to interest, in an annoying way. This is crucial because she is, of course, dead—but more alive than any other human being has ever been. She is, it hardly needs pointing out, God. Or perhaps not.

(Empty stage except for a full-size replica of a Spitfire. The ANNOYING OLD LADY gets out of the Spitfire and addresses the audience.)

ANNOYING OLD LADY

When I was a young girl—well, not young, exactly—and what is young anyway? As if angels who dance on the edge of a pin could see into the eyes of a young girl with bow legs. So to say.

(brightly, with a don't-eat-my-spinach laugh)

I had this dress—well, not a *dress,* per se, but more of a *frock* that just covered the very first rumblings of my mammalian womanhood, the inaugural spatial metamorphosis which would change forever my relationship with my chest and erupt gradually and finally with the appearance of my two fine breasts. . . . Where was I? Oh yes— when I was a young 'un, it seemed to me, in the private resources of my interior movie, that people, that is to say, adults, were relating to me as if I was a dog. Yes, a dog. Specifically, a bitch. Because I *was* a bitch—oh yes.

(a choked laugh with a tinge of melancholy happiness)

And then they gave me a dog. Well, not a dog, exactly. It *was* a dog. A catty dog. A catatonic dog. A cat. It was a cat. Yes, I'm almost sure it was a cat. But it was one of those cats that are, you know—dogs. We called it "Cat."

(a little spasmodic chortle, with a hint of Château Lafitte '82)

And I loved this dog as if it were my sister. And it was my sister. My little sister Cat. And every day I'd come home early from school and feed my little sister dog Cat. I'd feed it scraps from my lunch. Until one day my mother, whom we all called "the Duke," said to me, "Today, you annoying little girl, watch very carefully what I am about to do." And she went out to the driveway where little Cat was lying on the warm asphalt, got into her car—a 1948 Studebaker— and ran over my dog. On purpose. In front of my little girl eyes.

(rememberingly)

The dog's head splattered across the asphalt, rather decoratively, I thought, the red blood dripping like a—picture something poetic—into the gutter in the street. And I remember thinking— yes, I remember this distinctly, as if it had happened yesterday, "Well . . . There it is then." And I went inside.

(proudly hesitant)

And that was the day I grew up and became a woman, with eventual breasts. That was my baptism, my circumcision, the day I was, metaphorically speaking, sent out into the woods to become a man. Or in my case, a woman—as you can plainly see.

(brightly)

As you can *plainly* see in the brightest shine of day.

(two seconds pause)

"Shine of day"—Oh no. No no, that won't do. That won't do *at all*.
> *(she begins making odd hand gestures)*
Because growing up is all we can do.
> *(Is this a semaphore or what?)*
Anyway, that was the day of my thingamajig. My whatchamacallit. And I began having the most *extraordinary* dreams. And sometimes it was my mother, the Duke, driving over the dog, and sometimes it was the dog driving over my mother. Or the dog running over the dog, or my mother running over herself. But there was always a dog involved—that's the important thing. That's *very* important, so please take note. Please take note and *pay attention*. Because this is important—as is everything. And don't you forget it, Buster.

(The Spitfire disappears. STALIN comes on stage.)

STALIN
(awake but asleep)

Dasbidanya!

ANNOYING OLD LADY
(completely deaf, but intoxicated in the manner of someone who has just had two shot glasses of grape jelly)

Are you him?

STALIN
(as if singing in Swahili)

Yes.

ANNOYING OLD LADY
(as if her life depended on it, which it doesn't, but it does)

Stalin?

STALIN
(homosexually straight)

Yes.

ANNOYING OLD LADY
(pretending to smoke as if she were a small suitcase)
And what kind of metaphor is that supposed to be?

STALIN
(riveted but disinterested)
I am not a metaphor. I am Stalin.

ANNOYING OLD LADY
(to audience, conspiratorially, with a tinge of sadness, as if speaking to a small child or a large apple)
I always thought this would happen.

STALIN
(questioningly, from the POV of a medium-sized piece of wood)
I don't really exist. But here I am anyway!

ANNOYING OLD LADY
(virginally confused)
In my mind's eye I can still see my father driving a tractor across my sandbox, my mother driving her Studebaker over my dog, Aunt Agnes—who we always called Felix, for obvious reasons—yes, Felix, blowing up the local library. It was some childhood, as you can imagine.

(STALIN exits. We see a blue waterfall over an exact replica of the Duomo in Florence in 1:20 scale. The Duomo bursts into flames and changes into a large Plexiglas cube, ten feet on each side. We hear far-off barking. SOUSED MAN comes out of the cube.)

SOUSED MAN
Don't you see, Dearest, I'm in love with the dog. It's a ridiculous thing, I know, but there you are. The heart wants what it wants. The heart knows not from Woody Allen.

ANNOYING OLD LADY
(spectacularly shy)
Oh, Soused Man, you are the limit.

(The NAKED MAN runs on stage. He is very handsome and is naked and doesn't have any clothes on.)

NAKED MAN
(haltingly, as if he can't quite remember his lines)
We are never so alone in the world as we are in a room with a thousand people. Am I not right? We feel the connections in low wattage, we parse our personal moments in meticulous subtraction, ogling the freeway from afar.

(NAKED MAN exits. A twenty-foot dog comes on stage. It is completely invisible—that is to say, it is there, but not there, seen by the characters and extremely real.)

SOUSED MAN
(Sherlock Holmes)

Time for Elevenses.

(He begins mixing cocktails.)

ANNOYING OLD LADY
(life is a sandwich)
Soused Man, I hope you realize that in England—from whence your morning custom originates—the preferred beverage is a soft drink, not a hard one.

SOUSED MAN

Improvising.
(he completes concocting the cocktail)
Nectar of the saints!
(toasts)
To Saint Jude—Saint of Combustible Victuals.
(he downs it in a single gulp)

ANNOYING OLD LADY
Saint Jude is the Saint of Lost Causes.

SOUSED MAN

Are you sure?

ANNOYING OLD LADY

(introspectively, as if realizing for the first time that life is nothing but a collection of random, absurd and slightly surreal events and that one's existence could well begin and end at the footlights of a stage, watched by a great number of invisible people who nonetheless are there and observing every second of her life with rapt attention and increasing intensity)
Maybe.

(An ARMLESS DWARF comes on stage and sings "La Marseillaise." SOUSED MAN looks up and sees the huge invisible dog.)

SOUSED MAN

Bad dog.

(two minutes silence)

Down, dog.

(twelve minutes silence. Invisible dog disappears)

Dog dead.

(Twenty-six minutes silence. Lights fade. End of play)

JOHN UPDIKE

RABBIT ROCKS

Harry Angstrom doesn't quite know what to make of the call. It's Al Schacter, an old friend from his high school back in Brewer, Pennsylvania. Schacter's starting a "man band." "We'll show those kids," says Al.

"Show them what?"

"That rock 'n' roll is a man's business. I'm sick of all these 'N Syncs and Backstreet Boys, Rabbit. Whatever happened to music with balls?"

Rabbit has no idea what happened to music with balls. He doesn't even know what happened to the keys to the Celica. He remembers vaguely leaving them next to the box of Ring Dings in the kitchen, but he can't find them. The house looks out over the manicured lawns of Delean, Florida, and it's lovely and tidy, but he really never thought he'd end up in Florida, the "retiree" state. Still, here he is, in his mid-sixties, retired and playing golf nine times a week.

He reaches for another Ring Ding, stuffing it full in his mouth before Janice walks in the living room. "Have you seen the *TV Guide?*" she asks Rabbit. She's addicted to the soaps and the silly daytime talk shows that Rabbit finds depressingly lowbrow. She used to be thin and beautiful, lithe and tan, Rabbit thinks, but now the sun has aged and freckled her skin and worse, she just doesn't seem to care, wearing her pink Florida "fat pants" with the elastic waistband.

"No," says Rabbit.

"Are you eating again?" She doesn't even wait for an answer, but bends over to look for the *TV Guide* under the unread *Architectural Digest*s she thinks add a touch of class to the Pier One coffee table. Rabbit can't help noticing how fat her ass has become, so big he can picture a sign saying WIDE LOAD over her rear. Rabbit's mind wanders to the girls he sometimes watches on *MTV Rocks* and *Summer Dance Party*—nubile young things in low-rider pants and baby T-shirts that promote their rambunctious breasts. Maybe being in a "man band" wouldn't be so bad.

Rabbit calls Al.

"Yeah? You thought about it, huh?"

"It's interesting, but I'm not sure. I mean, I don't sing or play an instrument."

"That's the beauty part. It doesn't matter anymore! Have you seen this guy Moby? It's all machines. He just presses a button and mumbles into a microphone. And let me tell you, this Moby is no George Clooney."

"I'm no George Clooney, either," says Rabbit. He remembers when he thought he was George Clooney, sleeping with every woman in the neighborhood—including his own daughter-in-law. Those were the days.

"Believe me, next to Moby, you're John Travolta and Leonardo DiCaprio rolled into one."

Rabbit wonders what that would look like. But even Travolta is getting a little roly-poly these days. It's difficult. You eat just one box of Ring Dings a day, and after a couple of weeks you look like you're carrying twins.

"Come on up, we can figure it out. I've got Fred Benzwick interested too."

Freddy Benzwick? The man must smoke a pack a day—and that

was a decade ago when Rabbit knew him from the Brewer Chamber of Commerce, when Rabbit owned a Toyota dealership and Benzwick ran a hardware store on Clairmont Avenue. Now Freddy must have at least one foot in the grave. Rabbit tells Al about his reservations.

"That's true," says Al. "But he still has hair. I figure we need at least one guy with a good head of hair."

Restored Rabbit

Al meets Rabbit at Scranton Airport. Rabbit's surprised by Al's weird getup—a pair of those baggy jeans and a Tommy Hilfiger football jersey like the black kids wear in the hip-hop videos. Rabbit thinks he looks absurd, but maybe that's how the music business works—you wear the uniform. He offers him a Twinkie from the box he brought with him from Orlando.

"No, thanks," says Al. "Wow."

"What?"

"No, it's just that . . . you put on a bit more weight than I realized."

"I'm just big-boned," says Rabbit, stuffing another Twinkie whole into his mouth. "But I carry it well," he says, mumbling through the cream-filled, phallic sponge cake.

"Whatever."

Rabbit follows Al to his car parked in the garage. He's surprised—it's a Nissan Xterra. Everyone has an SUV now, but this is a young person's car. "What MPG do you get on this thing?"

"I have no idea," says Al.

The next day they start practicing in the basement of Al's ranch house, which Rabbit finds depressing with its peeling walls and threadbare carpet. Fred Benzwick joins them too, and they take turns pressing the button on the Macintosh iBook, seeing who can do it with the right kind of "Beckian" (Al's word) panache. Rabbit wins this contest—he darts his finger at the laptop and then taps the key with what Al calls "a perfect combination of irony and earnestness."

They practice a few dance moves, stealing a couple from what they remember of music videos they've seen on TV. Rabbit even incorporates a couple of basketball gestures, in a nod to his illustrious youth: he mimes dribbling on the spot and then leaps up and spin-throws the phantom ball for a midcourt three-pointer.

But what's the right name? They haggle over it, considering Gag Reflex, Twinkie Defense (Rabbit's suggestion), and Denture Deluxe. Al prefers Montrose—it's a little more serious than Moby as well as an homage to *The Full Monty,* the only film anyone can think of that featured a bunch of overweight middle-aged guys and still made over sixty million dollars. Democracy wins out; Fred likes Montrose too, so that's the name they use.

Rabbit on Ritalin

The booming nineties have turned Brewer into a town of unmistakable affluence, with a Gap, Starbucks, Barnes & Noble—even a Victoria's Secret in the Haverford Mall.

Montrose's first gig is at the high school gym, which Rabbit remembers well from his teenage years, but this is changed too. Rabbit marvels at the digital scoreboard, the sleek rows of bleacher seats, the huge Pepsi ads. They play some tracks from their new self-burnt CD: "Quaker Girl," "Nexium Orgy," "High Cholesterol," "Mortgage Man," and "Don't Get Me Started." Rabbit charges around the stage, patting his beer belly and cupping his crotch. The audience—a mixture of high school students and their bewildered parents—laugh at his antics.

"Give him some Ritalin!" shouts a kid in the front row. This gets a big laugh. Rabbit extravagantly mimes popping a pill, and the crowd bursts into enthusiastic applause.

Montrose gets booked for six more high schools. Word is out. At every high school they play, local press coverage builds until the act is welcomed on the front page. MTV sends a crew down to cover the self-proclaimed "man band," and the novelty attracts national attention. Fan sites pop up all over the Internet, with domain names like weluvmontrose.com and montrosia.net.

Before each gig, the men drink Gatorade and take their pills (Zocor, Zoloft). "Ritalin," jokes Rabbit, swallowing a multivitamin capsule. Even though each set is barely forty-five minutes long (even with them playing certain tracks twice), it still exhausts Rabbit and his bandmates. And they're still all younger than Bill Wyman. "How does he do it?" asks Rabbit.

"He's retired," says Al.

"Wimp."

Rabbit Is Really Randy

The Montrose video, directed by Spike Jonze, enters heavy rotation on VH1. It's a ripoff of *The Full Monty* and gets added publicity when the film's producer sues the band.

In Chicago, two young women, the Plaster Daughters of Chicago, invite Montrose back to their apartment for some historical mementos. Following in the tradition of their mothers, whose plastic handiwork of rock phalluses of decades past adorn the shelves, the Plaster Daughters coax their late-middle-aged pop stars erect and craft the figures. Rabbit, waiting his turn, peruses the statuettes. "Look, Hendrix wasn't that big."

"Mom said he was just fine," says one of the Plaster Daughters.

When it's Rabbit's turn to impale the bucket of white goo, he's already at full mast, excited by the heady scene.

"Hey, Rabbit," says Al. "We're gonna be right up there with Jim Morrison and Clapton."

There are more traditional groupies in other cities—college girls who just invite themselves into the limo after the gigs, trotting right after the group into their hotel suite. Wordlessly they peel off their skimpy clothes and unbutton the bandmates' pants. "You're the Full Monty guys, right?" Rabbit is amazed at the blithe manner with which their bestow blow jobs—the base currency of rockdom.

The heady mixture of drugs (Geritol, Zoloft, and Viagra) and sex (blow jobs, mostly, plus a fair amount of voyeurism) signaling to

Rabbit that the band has truly arrived. (They also get action figures by Mattel.)

Montrose is featured on the covers of *Dunky, Slam, Folio, Celebriweek,* and *Yahoo.* David Letterman has them read a Top 10 List ("Top 10 Reasons Man Bands Will Replace Boy Bands"—too pathetic to include here), and Howard Stern makes fun of them on live radio.

But it's all worth it. For the first time in years, Rabbit experiences the same ecstasy he felt playing basketball in high school or smelling the interior of a new Corolla when he ran a Toyota dealership. At the American Stars & Stripes Awards (broadcast on the E! entertainment channel), Rabbit meets his idol Jack Nicklaus, who has no idea who he is.

Watch Out, You Silly Wabbit

At the outdoor Greek Theater in L.A., where Montrose is opening for Leo Sayer and Sha Na Na, Rabbit looks out at the fawning middle-aged fans and their sulky kids, and he presses the button on the iBook, starting up the drum 'n' bass. He grabs a microphone and starts mumbling the lyrics of "Don't Get Me Started," his voice filtered and treated beyond recognition until it sounds like a moped without a muffler.

"Don't forget your Ritalin," he intones melodramatically into the microphone—his signature line. The crowd roars. Rabbit mimes a three-point throw, leaping up and tripping on a speaker cable. He falls into the front row—right into the familiar lap of a cartoon-blue sundress from Filene's Basement. It's Janice.

"Hello, Janice," Rabbit says. His right leg hurts like hell.

Janice doesn't say anything.

Rabbit Recovers Remarkably

"It's a compound fracture, so I should have the thing on for about six weeks," says Rabbit. He and Janice are sitting at Morton's, a trendy old-time industry eatery on Hollywood Boulevard. Rabbit's right leg is in a cast.

"Look, I think you're making a real fool of yourself," says Janice. "Cavorting up there like a nineteen-year-old."

"It's a statement."

"Of what? Middle-aged losers can be made fun of on TV, just like young people?"

"We're bringing back the man band."

"Who do you think you are, Led Zeppelin?"

"We might get our own cartoon series," says Rabbit excitedly. "As soon as the cast comes off, we're touring Australia and New Zealand, and then maybe doing the half-time show at the Super Bowl."

"You're a joke. They're calling it Lame Rock."

Rabbit rolls the term over in his mind. "I like that."

Carrot Top and Paula Jones approach their table. "Hope the leg isn't hurting too much," says the orange-haired stand-up comic. "You guys are really the shit."

"Thank you," says Rabbit. "You're shit too."

After they leave, Rabbit turns to Janice and says, "Paula Jones was much homelier than I expected. What did you think?"

Janice leans over and pecks Rabbit on the cheek. Then she stomps her foot hard on Rabbit's cast and storms off. Rabbit passes out.

Rabbit Realizes

When Rabbit awakes, he's doesn't know where he is. It looks like a short story, maybe a novella. He remembers that he actually died ten years ago, of a heart attack in Florida, but then he was still living with Janice, who was getting fatter, and his son, the nervous Nelson, continued to visit them with his bickering family.

He died, but the chapter wasn't over. There were still many R-words to describe his latest adventures. "Rabbit Gets a Rifle." "Rabbit's Rash Needs Radiation," Rabbit Is a Reactionary Racist," "Rabbit Radicalizes," "Radio Rabbit," "Rocket Rabbit," "Rocky Mountain Rabbit."

Rabbit had won two Pulitzer Prizes without even knowing it. He was a good-luck charm, a talisman, a trip to the bank. Theoretically, he could go on clashing with his family and the indignities of old age and the insults of contemporary culture for years. After all, he lived in the present tense.

Rabbit Buys a Robot

Oh, this is funny . . .

WILLIAM
BURROUGHS

NAKED BRUNCH

It was daylight when I walked into the Jones Diner and sat down on a metal stool next to a beef jerky who had grassed me two weeks before. It was mostly marmites and Jeebies (note: "Jeebies" is an English term for "Holycakes") at the Jones Diner on Great Jones and Lafayette, a strictly horse crowd (note: "horse" is a large quadruped with a mane, tail, and hooves. Latin name: *Equus caballus*). Mr. Jones himself was there at the griddle, as usual not comprehending anything (something was going on, but he didn't know what it was). "How about them Holes?" he said, staring up at the ancient TV hanging from the ceiling.

"Did you do it?" a man asked me. I looked around. It was Captain Plutarch of the Orgasmo Studio.

I'd just come from Orgasmo on Bond Street where I'd done some exterminating. It was a bad scene—they had cats the size of rats. I'd thrown out all the soft pillows and balls of string, and put arsenic in the Kal Kan. "That should keep them away for a week or so," I told the captain. "But once you've got cats, there's not much you can do about it."

An orange calico jumped up on my lap. "Mr. Jones, I could kill this one with a fork if you want, pro bono. Whaddaya say?"

Mr. Jones looked around slowly and shrugged. He was still busy watching the Ace-Hole game. "Nah. That's just Mason. But thanks. Maybe next time."

Two men in gray fedoras came into the diner, clearly patrol orcs from Yass-Waddah. I thought it best to scoot.

"Wait a minute, pal," said the first orc, barring my way. "Didn't we see you at the library last week drilling holes in a copy of Hammett's *The Thin Man?*"

"Not me, Officer," I said.

"Sure looked like you," pealed the second orc.

"Well, I look like a lot of questionable types. People frequently mistake me for a child molester, but in fact I'm just an exterminator, sir. Gotta get rid of the cats."

"Whaddaya have against the detective genre, anyway?"

"Nothing, sir."

"Did you check out a copy of *Gray's Anatomy* and return it with the pages cut up?"

"No, sir. Why would I want to do that?"

"All of the male, ahem, *genitals* had been removed."

"Must have been a mistake in the printing."

"Did you then *heglijib contajamjudig . . .* ?" The orc started melting, his words dripping like liquid out of his mouth, and I could smell the protoplasm, which was like a three-day-old dog carcass. Suddenly, he stuck a finger in his eye and pulled out a scrotal egg. *My God, he's from the Interzone!* I dove into his stomach and swam through a wet squid-ink cloud of ectoplasm, landing on an empty street in Tangier. Around a corner I encountered a group of small brown Arab boys beckoning me with outstretched arms. I tossed them some coins. They picked me up and carried me to a villa nearby, up twelve flights of stairs and into a huge apartment full of throw pillows where they stripped off my clothes and mercilessly engaged in Interzonal perversion with me for several days.

I woke up hunched over a small toilet in a small room with white tiles. After wiping myself off, I buttoned up and opened the stall door. It was the men's room at the New York Public Library. I stumbled out of the building and hailed a cab.

· · ·

When I got home, my wife was standing against the wall in her underwear. I'd forgotten I was married.

"Hey, Lover," she said. "Where the hell have you been?"

"I was, uh . . ."

"I missed you. For a faggot you sure are a good fucker."

This was true.

"Let's play William Tell," she said, placing an apple on her head.

"Not tonight, dear, I'm exhausted. I've been shooting up and exterminating since nine this morning."

"Come on," she purred. "Just one shot."

I had to admit it was tempting—I mean, there she was, a woman in her underwear with a damn apple on her head. She began humming the William Tell overture. I took out my Colt 45, shakily pointed it at the apple, and fired.

The police were very nice about it. On the minus side, I was a heroin addict and sexual deviant who had just killed his wife. But on the plus side, I was heir to the Burroughs Adding Machine fortune. On balance, they agreed, it pretty much evened out. "Just don't do it again," said the captain with a wink.

"Don't worry, sir—I am *never* getting married again."

They all hugged me at the ceremony that commemorated the new private gym I was going to build for Precinct 9. But I was beginning to feel the rumbling effects of the protoplasm again. I had to get away from law enforcement. The streets sagged and the sky was flaking over the Lower East Side, turning buildings into wet cardboard. The air smelled of burning cinnamon. I needed a fix—bad.

I copped a blip from a snorc in Washington Square and then squibbed over to the Jones Diner to see if the new batch of Wild Boys had come in. There they were, most of them thirteen or fourteen years old, all chained up naked on the wall next to the chalkboard menu.

"What'll it be, Bill?"

"Um . . . Everyone looks so good today. Can I have the Number Three Breakfast Special?" I said, eyeing the young blond hanging over the griddle.

"Too late for breakfast, Bill. It's after eleven."

"Then make it brunch. (Note: "Brunch" is a European term for a meal that combines breakfast and lunch.) "I'll take the number three, over easy."

Mr. Jones took down the blond kid and tossed him on the grill. "What about home fries?"

"Sure."

"How's the wife?"

"Don't even go there," I said with a wink.

Mr. Jones smiled. "I know just what you mean," he said, as he flipped over the kid and turned up the heat.

SALMAN RUSHDIE

THE SATANIC NURSES

Until it was withdrawn from publication due to the ire of the American Medical Association and the British Union of Hospital Workers, The Satanic Nurses *brought Salman Rushdie more notoriety than he had ever experienced before. This excerpt from the novel's opening is its first sanctioned appearance since the lifting of the Fatwa and Rushdie's being hired as the host of the reality game show* Danger Quest.

Before the ground opened up, before the sky was on fire, before the silver birds slid into the buildings like knives into cake, people walked as per usual, they worked as per usual, they ate and breathed and slept, as if life was normal, as if the world was not about to explode.

We live in the in-between, the other place, the un-world that is but is not, that is almost but not quite. And yet— when these two worlds collide, be not at that coordinate but there shall be fires that shall be hotter than hell, insidious hell, and then some.

My name is Orpheus F. Kennedy and I am 199 years old. I was born of the fire of Osiris in Bombay, before the time of the horseless carriage and the birds of death. I am the maharishi of the satanic nurses, and in the mysterious dust of my fingernails lies the fate of the earth.

I fell from the sky when Pan Am Flight 109 shook and shuddered and ruptured into burning rain over Finland. I was the only one who lived, the designated survivor, snowboarding through space, landing in a lake. I walked out of that lake naked as the day I was born, unscathed, unfazed, unfathomable, reborn, baptized, but with my memory destroyed. I named myself, I gave myself age, history, and personality. I bestowed upon myself a magnificence of which even the satanic nurses recognize as the true being, one of ones—and zeros. We run an accounting business. We account for everything.

But who was I? Milton Berle? Mick Jagger? Gianni Versace? Elton John? Why can I sing like a rock star, make jokes like a comic, design clothes that can be sold in the trendiest chain boutiques?

On one of my customized Fender Rhodes I tap out in Morse code the instructions to the bad nurses. They are to spread doubt, dissension, and dissonance throughout the Western world, to apply pressure to fresh wounds, to *wake us up.*

How dare the world sleep, tucked into its bosom and then wake to suck on the teet of its own complacency? How dare young girls, with their budding breasts and the oiled clefts between their legs, not know of the cruelties and aggression that await them? How dare young boys play unmolested and ignorant of the torn flesh that is their future?

How dare the people breathe, the animals run, the night turn into day?

But it dares. And so we visit the nurses of Station 911, who crouch at the start of a black dream, who wait with watches synchronized, with eyes peeled, with fingers itching, trembling on the trigger. The angels of death can change this world with a flick of a switch, a cut of a wire, the press of a button.

In London, two waitresses at the Hyde Park Hotel are taking their coffee break. "Be a pussycat and toss me a fag," says Marge to Mildred, as they sit on the rusty ladder on the fire escape. Marge luxuriates in her exuberant hair, in which Föno, the great Sri Lankan rock star, ejaculated last night. She combs a couple of ringed fingers through it, catching some of the snowlike flakes, the residue of their brief encounter. "Some Dionysian shindig last night," she says. "We raised the roof."

"I feel a foreboding," says Mildred. "Did you feel that?"

"Feel what?"

"Feel the appearance of bad nurses?"

In Manhattan, Sammy and Ed, two construction workers building the Tripe Tower at the corner of Mad and Fifth, salute each other with Styrofoam cups of coff. They stand on the girder at the sixty-second floor, perched as if on a sliver of thin air. "To the Apex of Tripe," says Sammy.

"The Epitome of Tripe," says Ed.

They clink cups and down their coff. The city looks cinematic beneath them, soft and colour-drained. All that is real is Tripe: the vast steel cage and slabs of concrete, a Babel inching its way towards God.

"Do you hear something?"

"Like what?"

"I don't know. A rumbling or something . . ."

"No, but I can see what looks like a couple of rotten nurses down there hacking away at an ATM with a sledgehammer."

In a ghetto in Karachi, Tariq, an eleven-year-old street scamp with a one-inch scar on his forehead in the shape of Pakistan and a soul as old as the Mahabharata, steals a bread roll off a cart. The merchant, one-eyed and with a face covered in scabs, grabs Tariq's hand, shaking the bread roll free. *"I will have you thrown in jail for this!"* he says.

A roar is heard from the far end of the street. It sounds like a regiment of despicable health-care workers.

The satanic nurses allow wounds to fester, bedpans to go unemptied, hospital food to remain inedible. They say, "This shouldn't hurt," then it hurts like a bastard. They demand reams of annoying paperwork to be filled out, and then make sure your insurance claim isn't honoured or even processed. They don't care when the emergency button is pressed, instead they make long-distance personal telephone calls from the nurses' lounge. They make fun of your hospital gown. They make you pee into a small paper cup.

"Good morning, Salman. And how are we feeling today?"

"We?"

"Let's take a look at your blood pressure, shall we?"

"Shall we?"

"Do you know why you're here?"

"Because of the satanic nurses?"

The nurse laughs. "Oh, that's precious, that is. I'll have to remember that one. Salman, you're here because your overwrought writing has exhausted you. You're suffering from megalomania and acute narcissism. You think the world revolves around you."

The world revolves around me. The thick crust of the earth splits like an avocado pit and swallows me whole. I grow and breathe and pulse within the sacred heart of the earth, my penis plugged into a catheter gives life and essence to the rivers, my fingers grasp the sands of the deserts, my eyebrows arch like mountains, my eyes watch from the bed of the seas.

Hey, when is it lunch around here, anyway?

JOYCE CAROL OATES

LIST OF WORKS
(As of press time)

I'm a Zombie
Guy Crazy
We Were the Bugzonics
Where Was I?
Foxfart
I'm Stuck in the Cupboard
Puddles (Poems)
Because I Wrote It and It Is There
Effluzia
Do Me If You Will
On Boxes: Observations
Under Boxers
Wonderbra (Odes)
Thems (Fictions)
Processed Words
Coming to a Bookstore Near You
I Just Wrote Another One
Hold On, I Just Got Out of the Shower (and Other Essays)
I'll Get It to You Thursday
With Shuddering Frequency

I'm Another Zombie
Untitled Novel
I Wrote It Anyway
Fast Opinions
A Quick History of the American Civil War (12 Volumes)
Stuck in Traffic (Poems)
I Thought You Said "Civil War," Sorry (and Other Essays)
Waiting in the Dentist's Office (and Other Poems)
The Prolix Saga (4 Volumes)
Dictions (Fictions)
The Pendletons of Puddlesfield
The Puddlesfields of Pendleton
Well F★★k Me Sideways
I Like That Brad Pitt (and Other Observations)
Whodathunkit (I Did)
On Being Black (Essays)
Monica's Diary
I Am Kennedy (Eat Me)
Yalees Spit (and Other Plays)
Lint in My Pocket (Poems)
Penny Arcadia (Ephemera)
O. J. Simpson Is My Suitcase
James Joyce Carol Oates (Dreams)
Mike Tyson Electric Vaudeville
The Complicated Saga (5 Volumes)
Dental Cleavage: Thoughts on Lookism
Lisa Gotthead Is Thirteen Years Old Tomorrow
I Think I Stepped in Something (No, It's You)
Princess Diana's Last Buttered Moments (10-Play Cycle)
Correspondence (12 Volumes)
Selected Telephone Calls
Collected Menus
The Diary of Otto Frank (withdrawn)
Fiction Affected
Afflicted Affections
I Can't Stop Thinking About That Ben Affleck (and Other Observations)
(sic) (Thoughts)

Hitler's Panties (Poems)
Cleopatra's Penis (Lyrics)
Churchill's Titties (Libretto)
Contractual Obligation Novel
Is That the Time? (Stories)
I'm Thinking of Remodeling the Kitchen (and Other Observations)
I'm a Believer: Musings on the Monkees
I'm a Zombie Again
On Wrestling
On Baseball
On Knitting
On Sleeping
On Onanism
On or About June 24th
Tracy Bickle's First Orgasm
John Updike's Stutter (An Appreciation)
Pantaloons (Sudden Fictions)
Gas Station Attendants Are My Weakness (Stories)
Celluloid Cellulite: Older Women in the Movies
Whorehol (Art Criticism)
Moz/Art (Music/Art Criticism)
Danny Kaye Was Pretty Talented, You Gotta Admit (Appreciation)
DVD/DDT: On Poisonous Popular Culture
Roach Motels (Travel Essays)
Popular Mechanics (Friends in Suburbia)
No, I Ordered the Chicken Marsala (Thoughts on Dining)
On a Roll (Restaurant Reviews)
I Think I'm Allergic to Peas (Musings on Food)
Bedpans: Hospital Experiences
On the Mend: Observations on Getting Well
Why Haven't You Called Me Lately? (and Other Whines)
Married to My Work
Tome (Novel)
I'm a Different Zombie, Completely Unlike the Other Ones
A Catholic Girlhood
On Being Jewish
Muslim Weekends
Buddhist Mistress

WASPism
The Norton Book of Knitting (Editor)
Remembering 'Nam (Sam I Am)
Presidential Platform
Winning Is the Only Thing (Essays)
Losing Is No Disgrace (Poems)
Hubert H. Humphrey: A Biography (3 Volumes)
The Life of Humbert Humbert (6 Volumes)
I'm Writing as Fast as I Can (Lyrics)
French Agricultural Systems of the 16th Century: An Introduction
Selected Double Acrostics
Woody Allen Broke My Carburetor (A Gothic Romance)
Look for This Space (Selected Criticism)
The Oates Book of Eye Design
The Extremely Long Saga (6 Volumes)
Faster Than Stephen King (7 Novellas)
Dress Patterns
Interstate Maps (Editor)
This Just In . . .
Shrill Screeds
Collected Leaflets (1964–86)
The Oxford Book of Dog Grooming (Editor)
Boswell's Life of Johnson's Life of Boswell (Essays)
Internest
The Complete E-Mails (3 Volumes)
The Oates Bran Muffin Cookbook
Blistered Fingers (Memoir)
Harvard Schmarvard (Collected Graduation Speeches)
Remainder Bin (Essays 1968–98)

JOHN IRVING

TWO CHEERS FOR LEON BIXBY

Were it not for a monkey killing a nun with a fork in an Automat, Oklahoma would now be part of Arkansas, and I would not be the billionaire animal dentist that I am today. It happened in Chicago on V-E Day, and as Harry Truman (not *the* Harry Truman, but "a" Harry Truman, though he was certainly "the" to me) used to say, "Tufark—there's three sides to every coin."

Yes, Tufark is my name, and how it became so is a 366-page story in itself. A further 292 pages will be devoted to the tale of the bear that ate my pajamas and was subsequently named honorary lieutenant-colonel of the 181st Airborne Division (the only non-human to be so honored).

That nun in the Automat was my grandmother, and that monkey had nothing to do with the bear. Still, Arkansas is a state I've always admired, and though money has never meant anything to me, I was glad to be able to bail out Argentina and marry, if only briefly, the niece of Lee Harvey Oswald.

Yes, I'm a JFK assassination buff (aren't we all?), but Harry Truman was right when he told me, "Don't light the fuse if you can't get out of the way."

Oh, I lit the fuse all right—the chipmunk with the overbite

could tell you that. But animals need good teeth as much as the next guy, and I was happy to do root canal on Fidel Castro's crocodile. It's how I became a Communist.

That croc was Leon Bixby, who gives his name to this book. The difference between an alligator and crocodile, people will tell you, is that an alligator has a shorter snout and is tamer than a croc. But from a dental point of view, crocs have much better teeth, and more of them too. A croc is also the most soulful of reptiles, and he can sense your mood at thirty meters. If he senses you're depressed, for instance, he's more likely to try to eat you, which I consider kindness itself.

I know what you're thinking: A billionaire Communist? Castro and I used to laugh over this for hours. *Eres demasiado rico para ser comunista*, he'd say, chewing on a pencil (he'd long since sworn off cigars). His teeth, by the way, were nothing to write home about.

But Leon Bixby—there was a creature, milk chocolate brown, proud and resourceful. He used to look at me as if I were his own kin.

I was born Clarendon Henderson III, in a small outhouse in Suskutch, Missouri. Being young at the time, I can't recall the exact circumstances of my birth, but from family legend I understand that my mother (Pheral) didn't actually realize she was pregnant. Distraught at gaining so much weight, she'd been practically starving herself to maintain her trim figure. That morning, feeling a little woozier than usual, she stumbled to the outhouse and sat on the toilet for two hours, suffering from what she assumed was a particularly severe case of constipation (she'd been taking handfuls of laxatives for days). Finally she effused me into the toilet, luckily recovering from the shock quickly enough to reach down and retrieve me from the bowl. It was a striking (and rather rank) catharsis for both of us. The toilet was a cheap porcelain model then seen in outhouses throughout the Midwest. It was called the Clarendon. Henderson was my mother's name (she was unmarried). The number at the end of my name was a fancy—perhaps my mother's perverse joke after finding my Christian name on a toilet; there were no Clarendon Hendersons one and two. Technically my last name is "III," pronounced "The Third," so I should be addressed as Dr. The Third (and listed in the directory under "T").

But everyone knows me as Tufark—even Castro, who called me Señor True-Fart, his modest English extending farthest in British schoolboy humor. (He once told me his greatest regret in life was not going to Eton.)

If my grandmother, Sister Jude, could have foreseen me ministering to Communists and reptiles, she probably would have grabbed the fork from the monkey and done herself in. She was the most pious of capitalists with a deep hatred and distrust of animals. The one time she let her guard down, striking up a conversation with some circus folk at the Horn & Hardart on West 42nd Street, she was cruelly and fatally punished for it. Witnesses claimed it was a completely unprovoked attack, but looking at it from the monkey's point of view, a large, menacing figure covered mostly in black was suddenly shuddering and wheezing at him. That was how my grandmother laughed, people said, on the few occasions that she did so. She was a serious woman and had stopped in New York on her way to Washington to present her Arkansas finding. Back in Little Rock, in a box in the basement of the Carmelite Order of the Spherical Handshake, she'd found incontrovertible evidence that all the treaties with Arkansas and Oklahoma really referred to the same geographical area, but due to an early congressional oversight, they'd become popularly known as two different territories. I have in my possession this very document, and though I can't be sure of its authenticity, it looks real enough to me. Had it been brought to the attention of the government, it could have made for a funny-looking flag. Schoolchildren all across the nation would be charged with the unfortunate task of pulling stars off Old Glory. There would be fistfights in the corridors of Congress between representatives of the two delegations. Countless license plates would have to be destroyed.

Needless to say, the document never reached its destination, and Sister Jude met her maker at the Horn & Hardart. Normally, city editors live for such a freak confluence of disparate elements; in newspaper terms, the meeting of "nun," "monkey," "Automat," and "murderous fork" is like the lining up of the planets. But victory in Europe did not make for a slow news day, and her sad demise, which on any other day would have easily snagged the front page, was relegated to a small local news item at the bottom of page 16 of the *New York World*. By the time the sisters back in Arkansas discovered what had happened, Sister Jude had already been in a pauper's grave for two weeks. A collection was raised to erect a small monument in Woodlawn Cemetery to commemorate her would-be political mission, and I've visited this modest edifice. It lies not more than twenty feet from the grand cenotaph of Harry Houdini, giving Sister Jude a far tonier address in death than she ever had in life. It's an elegant little obelisk, but I must admit to taking some exception to the legend chiseled on its face: "She lived an exemplary, monastic life that should be an example to us all." *Exemplary?* Debatable. *Monastic?* Not quite. She did, after all, give birth to my mother, nine months after opening the door to a young Jehovah's Witness. Was the man lost? Why else would he have walked through the gate of a nunnery? But the 1930s were a tough time for everyone, and perhaps he felt he had nothing to lose.

I don't know the details of that secretive union. All I know is that my mother inherited Sister Jude's meager sense of humor along with a thirty-one-volume *Encyclopedia Americana* that was dropped off along with her at the orphanage. The reference set must have towered over her on the doorstep, and I picture this image, the stacks of encyclopedias and the infant—my mother, Pheral—in a concave basket, as resembling a nativity scene at the United Nations complex.

Perhaps it is that image that has given me my wandering spirit, my wanderlust. As Harry Truman—*the* Harry Truman—used to say: "If you can't stand the heat . . ." Well, you know the rest.

TONI MORRISON

BELABORED

Her stomach reeled, it shook—it quaked with an anger unnatural to an unborn thing. Suge placed her hands on her rumbling belly and tried to soothe her unruly tenant.

"Hush there, sweet Maybe-Baby. Yer gonna break my stomach. . . ."

Suge had been pregnant for nineteen years, since the days of the before-time, when she and the Jackson Brothers worked the land around the Neverland Ranch.

Baby Mama used to say that Suge should just do away with it, or pull it out, kicking and screaming, whatever its age. "Ain't right the baby's been in there so long. Should at least be payin' rent."

Her daughter, Detroit, the born one, seethed with a jealous rage for all the attention accorded the unborn one.

Suge, the daughter-sister of Baby-Mama and Sister-Baby, knew what had to be done. She had to stay in the house in case Maybe-Baby showed up in the middle of the night. It'd be no use if Maybe-Baby crawled out and got lost somewhere in the woods. No matter how big or old it was, it wasn't likely to show up with a terrific sense of direction. So every night Suge locked all the doors and shut the blinds. More than once Detroit had been locked out after stumbling home late from a night's carousing at a juke joint.

When she lived at Neverland, Suge had been the most desirable woman for miles around—on account of being the only woman for miles around. Michael Jackson, Boss Man of the Big House, was the youngest of five brothers who he'd forced out to work the ranch. They maintained the Ferris wheel and stoked the miniature train. They fed the animals at the zoo and swept the floor of the twenty-four-track recording studio. It was a tough life, made harder still by the monotonous dance steps they were forced to learn year after year, even though there was no one to see them.

And then Suge arrived, with Baby-Mama and Sister-Baby, two folks who may have been the same person, no one was quite sure— including Suge herself. She'd say things like, "When Baby-Mama was here, she used to—" And Detroit would interrupt, "You mean Sister-Baby?" And Suge would have to stop and think about it. "I guess," she'd say.

Detroit was born of one of the Jackson Brothers; Suge refused to say which one. The others were left to fuck sheep and then cows and then (briefly) horses, and then sheep again. No one liked to speak about Mister Michael, who insisted on being called the King of Pop. He was an odd little man who went around the ranch attached to a baby chimpanzee, and he invited young boys from miles around to come over and play. He sure was one strange white folk.

Suge didn't want another baby born in such a world, and the fetus evidently agreed with her. But boy was it angry! It kicked her from within and left the radio on all night so Suge couldn't get to sleep. How did it get a radio in there? But that wasn't all. Sometimes Suge could smell the pungent odor of reefer and realized that Maybe-Baby was *smoking* in there. And there was giggling and laughing, and she realized further that Maybe-Baby had smuggled in some friends. Sometimes they seemed to get into fights, and Suge's belly rocked with the kicking over of furniture and once a smash that sounded like a destroyed television set. Suge tried to soothe Maybe-Baby by stroking her belly and singing to it old Motown songs.

"Motown used to be my town," said Detroit sullenly. "I remember when you used to sing to me." She was about to hit her sister-mama (or was she her mama-sister or just mama-mama?) with a pool cue when they both heard an odd series of dance steps outside and looked out the kitchen window to see old Jermaine J. shuddering to himself. He danced on to the porch where Suge came out to greet him.

"Well, if it ain't Action Jackson."

"Hello, Suge. You still pregnant?"

"You betcha."

"Seems like an awful long time to be pregnant. If you'd just let it come out, it'd be heading off to college by now."

"How're the brothers?"

Jermaine shrugged. "Don't see them nowadays. All gone our separate ways. Except His Royal Majesty the King of Pop. He's still at Neverland, nutty as ever. Now he wants to be called the Emperor Cow-Pow."

"Why?"

"Why? I dunno. Maybe he's into cowpunching. Who knows? He's nuts, I tells ya."

Detroit picked up the piano stool and threw it at Jermaine, who ducked just in time.

"Detroit, don't you throw a piano stool at Mister Jackson. What he ever done to you?"

Detroit didn't say anything, but skulked off to the woods to practice her accordion.

"That girl of yours need a good whippin'."

"Don't you talk to my daughter like that. She's been in a bad way ever since 'The Day the Music Died.'"

"You mean when Buddy Holly, Ritchie Valens, and the Big Bopper's plane went down in Clear Lake, Iowa, on February third in 1959?"

"That's it."

"For me 'The Day the Music Died' was when the King—the *real* King—kicked off on his gold toilet at Graceland and entered the Kingdom of Elvis," said Jackson.

Just then Suge's stomach surged and punched Jackson in the most private of parts, and he yelped in pain. "That belly of yours sure holds a mighty wallop," said Jackson, cradling his genitals. "I haven't been punched like that since Barbra Streisand made *Yentl*."

"Why, what happened then?"

"She punched me."

Suge was caressing her belly, trying to soothe Maybe-Baby. "He don't mean it," she said to her stomach. "He don't mean nothing by that. He just like Elvis, is all. What's wrong with that? Everyone cried the day Elvis died." Suge thought back to that day, when the sky was streaked in gray and it rained cold as glass. She had spent the day out back planting crabgrass, and she looked out to the field that had convulsed under the storm, turning the dirt into mud and then into a lake.

"You never said which one of us knocked you up."

"I know," said Suge, still thinking of the lake. The neighbors had named it Lake Wobegon, after their favorite cracker radio show.

"I'm pretty sure it wasn't me. I was more into sheep in those days. And Detroit don't look nothing like me." He could hear her accordion playing in the woods. It sounded like a duck being strangled repeatedly. "I always thought it was Mister Michael that knocked you up, even though he never seemed too concerned with girls. Even so, that's what I thought. He used to call you Billie Jean."

"That was Tito," said Suge. "Tito had the kindest hands. He's Detroit's father. But where is he?"

"I think he runs a gas station in Spotch, Mississippi, not far from Tupelo, where Elvis was born."

And then Suge's belly rocked and socked Jermaine hard, missing his jewels but catching him on the hip bone. "Shit, that belly got game!"

"It does that every time it hears the name of the King. You know—the real one—not, uh, Mr. Pop."

"Girl, what's that in your belly? Is it a demon? An angel? What is it?"

Suge turned quiet and looked reverentially up at the ceiling. "God whispered in my ear, the day Elvis died, and then I became big with child. For a very long time."

Jermaine whistled. "Woo-wee," he said. "Girl, sound to me like you need some TLC. You gotta fall, girl. You gotta fall into my arms. I'll catch you. That's what I'm here for. Fall, girl, fall—I'm for you."

Suge felt the knot in her head and the hunch in her shoulders began to melt. She felt the clenched rock inside her body crumble like a pile of wet sand—and she fell back.

Just then Detroit started up her accordion again, and Jermaine moved to close the window. Suge hit the hardwood floor with a bang.

"I thought you said you were gonna catch me," she said, looking up at Jermaine.

"Sorry, I got distracted." He closed the window. "Let's try it again."

"No siree. I may be a blimp, but I ain't no fool."

Jermaine moved to help her up, but she suddenly clutched her stomach and waved him away. "I . . . I think it's . . . time. . . ."

"Time for what?"

"Maybe-Baby . . . maybe won't be maybe much longer. . . ."

"Oh, no."

There wasn't time to get Suge upstairs, so Jermaine dragged her outside through the backyard and into the barn. He lay her down on the straw and ran off to get a transistor radio.

"Forget the radio," said Suge. "Just call Detroit."

By the time Jermaine returned with the radio and Detroit had come with her accordion, they beheld an amazing sight.

A fully dressed man walked out of the barn. He was a little pudgy, with large black sunglasses, long black sideburns, and a white jumpsuit, studded with rhinestones, which flared at the leg where his feet were sheathed in black boots with platform heels. "Aloha," he said, karate-chopping the air. "I'd like to do a little something I like to call . . . 'Are You Lonesome Tonight?' "

As he began singing, Suge appeared behind him, tired-looking, but a lot thinner. The sky had cleared, and a bright spotlight pierced the air and lit them in a halo of light, at 11 in the morning.

JAY McINERNEY

WHAT LIGHTS, WHICH CITY?

You are not the kind of guy who would be writing a book like this, but here you are, at two A.M., typing into your titanium Powerbook G4, and you cannot say that the terrain is entirely unfamiliar. It's another story about models and nightclubs, a melancholy narrator musing over a whiff of days gone by, before the latest stock market crash, when life was simpler, richer, more successful, with a few nods to your hero F. Scott Fitzerald. Some people have even remarked on a superficial resemblance: the strong jaw, the Celtic heritage, the midwestern childhood, the excellent hair. He too had spousal complexities and needed literary coal to stoke the engine of alimony. But your well is running dry and you need some new material.

You go out and flag down a cab piloted by a Jamaican smoking a spliff and blaring reggae on the cab's meager sound system.

"Where to, Caspar?"

You wonder if he calls all white people Caspar, and if this is the equivalent of you calling him Sambo. You ask him politely to turn down the music. He interprets this as a request to crank it up to the decibel level of a Boeing 747 achieving liftoff.

You decide to go to Supermarket, the latest club of the moment, situated in a former supermarket on Avenue D. You remember when this area looked like downtown Kabul after a couple of F-16s had left their calling cards. The bouncer—a sumo wrestler in a cheap Armani knockoff—bars your way. You can recall when there wasn't a single velvet rope in the city that didn't part for you instantly on sight, when you were the Moses of the midnight club crawl. But this Tarzan doesn't recognize you. You'd press the point, but he doesn't look like the *Esquire* type—more *Stuff* or *Maxim*. Luckily, a Phoenix (Leaf or Twig, you're not sure which) sweeps out of a limo and the velvet is unclicked just long enough for you to blur with the whoosh through the door.

Inside, several of the aisles have been removed, but the Specials signs still hang from the ceiling, advertising ghost promotions. A check-out counter serves as the bar and the meat section constitutes the coat check. You wonder if bourgeois utilitarianism turned into a symbol of elitist decadence is an irony that hasn't overstayed its welcome. Perhaps the hipper thing might be club kids just shopping at a supermarket during the day, checking the sales circular, cutting out coupons.

A cigarette girl pushes a shopping cart with her tobacco wares. Her face has the weary nonchalance of someone who has just come off shock therapy, and she wears a pair of Baby Gap jeans and a T-shirt that might better fit a hamster. In her navel is the requisite shrapnel and the flare of a pink tattoo stretches from her crotch. You smile at her and wonder if she recognizes you. And then you calculate that she was probably four years old when your first book came out.

"Care for a fag?" she says—which startles you (is it your suit that suggests an ally of Oscar Wilde?), until you remember reading somewhere (*Slate? Salon?*) that Cockney slang is in this year.

"Shut your fat gob, Guv'ner," you say politely in the best East End you can muster. She stares at you blankly, as if you had just spoken Pashtun.

The music that is being played has all the emotion of a CD-ROM drive. You don't understand the new pop tunes—either the jailbait Lolitas warbling their fuck-me ballads, or the dull totem drum 'n' bass, throbbing out of the speakers.

The drugs have changed too. The Bolivian marching powder

has been replaced by a little chemical lab disk, like a small communion wafer, which you suck into ecstasy—pacifier music, to which the platoon of professional mannequins bob in perfect formation and rhythmic boredom.

A girl with the elegant skeletal frame of an Auschwitz survivor approaches you. She too has metal in her mouth, lips, and chin, as if a box of paperclips had exploded in her face.

"Like, I know you," she goes.

"Thank you," you go.

"Like, you wrote that amazing book," she goes.

"Thank you," you go.

"About the handsome guy who cut up women," she goes.

"That wasn't me," you go. "That was Bret Easton Ellis."

"Oh yeah, right. So, like, whatever happened to him?"

"He died," you say, not entirely inaccurately.

Because it's true: Ellis died, along with Tama Janowitz, and you as well—the hip, eighties trifecta, when young writers were rock stars, just after young artists were rock stars, but before young models were rock stars, and then young directors were rock stars. Who were the rock stars now? Rock stars?

But there aren't any rock stars anymore. Kids sample other people's music and borrow other people's emotions. They spin records, making a stuttering cacophony of halting sound.

It has all changed. Everyone is younger now, the kids look barely out of high school. Nobody reads anymore. It's been a long time since hip fashion boutiques sold books at the counter, next to the shoes and hats. That is, *certain* books—the treasured few tomes that had captured the Zeitgeist, had caught lightning in bound signatures. The books looked like record jackets then. Now they look like magazine ads for Napa Valley cult wines, and CDs look like matchbooks from restaurants you can't remember going to.

Books used to be fashion accessories. Now they're just books.

Your cell phone throbs. You answer it. It's one of your ex-wives, you're not sure which one. You have enough former spouses to woman a basketball team, or maybe an all-wife band—the Menopausers or perhaps the Chemical Sisters. She is babbling on about money, and the lack thereof. You have to admit, she has a point: Why did you buy the horses, the houses, the wines, and wives? What did you need with the stud farm or the trimaran or the '66 Aston Martin?

The call thankfully cuts off, just as you were about to quote Fitzgerald's line about there being no second acts in American life. But you're determined to prove him wrong.

A small chap in a tweed suit seems to be attempting a negotiation with a young blonde. You overhear the words "assignation" and then notice the blank stare of the girl. You hear the word "friend of Jagger," and notice that the blonde's apparent catatonia remains unchanged. After the girl walks away and the man turns around, you see that it's your lawyer, Harold Duck, whom you call Duck.

"Hello, Duck."

"Oh, Jay. Nice to see you, Old Boy."

"What say you we blow this joint and find the adult table?"

You and Duck go out and get a cab to the "21" Club. The maître d' welcomes you effusively, leading you to a table by the men's room. As he's seating you, he says, "Nice to have you back, Mr. Lowe."

Duck orders a Johnny Walker Red—full bottle. You order an Henri Bonneau from Châteauneuf-du-Pape 1990 Réserve des Celestins. You notice that the sommelier's cummerbund is askew, and this detracts from the bouquet of the wine, a superb vintage with a lazy brunette pitchfork overhue.

Duck wheezes into his fist. You wonder if this is influenza or an ostentatious form of stage gout. You observe that new money has the postcoital blush of a quick fuck in a broom closet, whereas old wealth is all bored satiation.

"Muffy fell off his Mustang the other day," says Duck.

"I didn't hear," you go. "I was in London, actually."

"Really?"

"Yes. Saw Martin."

"Martin?"

"Amis. We were in the Groucho, eating bed-chippies with Hanif and Sal."

"Bed-chippies?"

"Kureishi and Rushdie."

"Oh."

"The British are crazy. They want to turn my last book into an opera or a sitcom."

"Hasn't that already been done?"

"Touché."

"You know, I'm, uh, I've been seeing Alison," says Duck. "You don't mind, do you?"

Alison is your second or third wife. You assumed someone had been dating her, but you never would have suspected Duck. Offhand, you don't see any problem with this—except that Duck is your lawyer and he's supposed to be representing you in the new divorce resettlement. Suddenly your ex-wife's recent demands make a little more sense.

"Of course not," you say.

The check arrives, on a little silver platter. It comes to $138. You notice Dick patting his pockets theatrically.

"I say, Jay. You couldn't front me for this one, could you? I seem to have misplaced my wallet."

Story of your life. Mr. Jones is down again, and Dr. Nasdaq's arteries are clogged. Nobody has any money.

You pay and take a cab down to the West Village, alone. Dawn is breaking through a fissure in the clouds. You wander the streets you used to know like the back of your hand. You smell bread, and suddenly it all comes back—your first apartment on Cornelia Street, with the smell of bread in the morning, when you'd come stumbling home after another night at Area or M.K. The eighties were long ago, when everything was simpler.

You realize that everything has to change. Everything has to go back to zero. Everything must be reinvented.

It's time to get married again.

MARTIN AMIS

STALKING MR. BELLOW

It begins with a quick phone call, words dancing in electricity, placed to windyville Chicago. Picked up on the twenty-third ring.

"Hello?" A voice from the cattle yards, Dreiser's ghost and Ben Hecht's surly drawl, the . . . "Hello!?"

"Hello, Saul. It's me, Martin."

"Who?" he says—a delicious, obvious wink. As if he doesn't know . . .

"Amis," I say with a laugh, sharing the joke.

Then, a long pause—as flat as the plains, as tall as the buildings that scrape the sky on Chicago's North Side, the wind descending off Lake—

"What do you want, Marvin?"

"Ha ha. I just need a little quotee, Saul."

"A what?"

"You know—a blurb. For my new book."

"What new book?"

And here I laugh, because of course he's joshing again, pretending he hasn't heard about *Electric Teeth: An Anti-Novel of the Millennium in Blank Verse*. (But is that the right title? Should it be *Earth's Enema*? Or *Time's Hollow*?) The proles know all about it, the dartners and dodgers, Joe Taxi Driver from Brooklyn, New York, in his

Italian schmatta and his sparkled togs, prowling through the caverns of the Lower East Village. I can hardly walk down First East Ave without hearing a newstander—one of those brave, type-happy Gutenbergians in their rug-rethinks—yell to me, "Howzit goin', Amis? Whuzzup?"

"Saul? Hello? Saul?"

Dear Saul,

Did you get the puppy? His name is Herzog. I hope it didn't get squashed in the mail. If so, just let me know and I'll send you another one. Chicago is great! When I hit Lake Shore Drive, I know I'm home, baby. I'm staying at the Hilton—Room 1215. Drop by!

Yours,
Martin

Dear Saul,

I can't help thinking that you might be trying to avoid me. I've been diligently waiting at Jimmy's Woodlawn Tap on Fifty-fifth Street for three days in a row. Briefly, on the second day (Thursday), I vacated my spot to take a leak. Could you have perchance dropped by then and missed me? (Since then I've brought a piss bottle to avoid such a reoccurrence.)

I feel we have a true bond. I'm the son you never had. You're the father I never had. We belong together in the true spiritual, literary sense.

Yours,
"Marvin"

Dear Saul,

I enjoy our correspondence and I think it is significant and instructive. I call you. You signify the call by pretending to avoid me. I wait for you in your local tap. You respond by not showing up—i.e., "unwaiting." I follow you to the supermarket. You take out a protection order against me, in effect "protecting" our unique relationship. I try to get into your apartment. You have me arrested. Our intellectual arm wrestling is "arrested" in mid-game. A draw. In any case, I am enjoying Chicago and am considering a chapter on it in one of my works in progress, *The Moronic Infatuation: Essays on*

America. I love the jingle-jangle of the shoe-monkeys, tub-happy in their omnivorous muff-diving and jazz-tenemention. As you see, I've caught the lingo. I *am* a Chicagonian—a windonian lakehack! I'm sick of old London and its small-minded teaheads. I have suffered the slings and arrows of invidious reviews, I have been banned from the Booker Prize, I have had my moral tracts torn asunder under notices with headlines like "Too Clever by Half." Half! I am not half! I am twice that and then some!

Anyway, drop me a line, stating point of view. While awaiting your response, I'm working on a couple of projects: *The Killer Effete: Gay Murderers and Murderees* and *Hactotems: The Serial Killer Assistants and Their Meanial Tasks*. I've dedicated them both to you, plus the new novel. Hope you don't mind. You the man, man! Looking forward to your RESPONSE.

> Your pal,
> Martin

Saul—

Look, man, you gotta help me here! I'm stuck in Joliet awaiting my arraignment and my publisher is bugging me for that quote. To make things easier, I've put together some sample blurbs you can choose from. Just check one off—or even spill some coffee on it and that'll denote your choice.

☐ "Martin Amis is the finest writer since James Joyce." (This is my personal favorite.)

☐ "Martin Amis is my only obvious literary heir. This book is terrific!"

☐ "Martin Amis is a genius! Any new book from him is a true event."

☐ "His best book by far! Amis is a genius!"

☐ "Great work! Amis deserves the Nobel Prize!"

> Thanks, man!!!
> Yours, Martin
> (i.e., "Marvin")

Dear Saul,

I appreciate your agreeing to drop the "charges," but I think the conditions are a little steep.

First of all, I was never "stalking" you, so I can't very well *stop* doing what I never did in the first place!

Secondly, to agree to stop trying to contact you in any manner could severely hamper our relationship. (I assume your lawyers came up with this demand. But please take a look at it; it isn't fair or feasible, for either of us.)

Thirdly, as I already explained, I didn't send you a "dead dog"—the pup just got slammed in transit (not my fault!), as did Herzog II (presumably—UPS is still trying to trace that one).

Fourthly, I resent being described in the affidavit as "a writer." Surely, after "Martin Amis," if any designation is listed, it should be "the writer." A small point, perhaps, but I think a significant one.

Fifthly, I didn't write *Lucky Jim* as you explained to the judge. That was my father.

Please call your lawyers off and let's settle this quickly and amicably.

> Sincerely,
> M. Amis (Inmate
> #5937721)

Dear Saul,

Obviously, I'd like to resolve this as soon as possible, and I'll agree to whatever settlement you suggest, as long as you give me a blurb. Simple as that. You can word it any way you like. Then I promise you'll never hear from me again.

> Ciao,
> Martin

"Martin Amis is a writer of distinct . . . and singular . . . talent."

> —Saul Bellow

PHILIP ROTH

ROTH UNBOUND

I got the call just as I was about to leave my apartment to meet some friends for dinner.

"Your pal is in trouble," said a voice I didn't recognize.

"What pal?"

The man told me. "You'd better come down here and pick him up." He gave me the details. It had to be a mistake, but I couldn't be sure. I'd been hearing rumors for weeks that the man was on the loose.

I called my friends and told them I wouldn't be able to make it that night and we'd have to reschedule. "Sorry. Something's come up," I said.

I took a cab to the Village and twenty minutes later walked into the Cedar Tavern.

I recognized him immediately. Older, of course, but it was him all right—the urgent jaw, the severe eyebrows, now gray. Hair just about gone. He was clearly drunk and had stumbled up to a couple of girls—college students, by the look of them—who were sitting at the bar, minding their own business.

"You know who I am?"

The redhead appraised him. "Mister Rogers?"

The man hacked out a laugh. "Mister Rogers is dead. I'm *Alexander Portnoy*."

Both the girls looked at each other and shrugged. "Congratulations," said the blonde.

"Oh come *on*. Don't they teach you anything in that idiotic college of yours? I'm *Portnoy*. Of the famous *Complaint*."

"Well, I hope you get it cleared up then," the redhead said. Both the girls laughed.

"*Portnoy's Complaint*—it sold like ten million copies."

Like? Portnoy was using *like?* I could remember when his vocabulary was better than that, when his exuberance was contagious, when he was outrageous and always fun to be around. But now, but this . . .

I ordered a glass of Pellegrino and sat at the bar, perpendicular to Portnoy and the girls so I could observe what was going on.

"I think my mother may have read that," the redhead was saying.

"She did?"

"Yeah, I think I remember seeing it in the bathroom."

"Really?"

"Didn't someone called Ross write it?"

"*Roth*. Hah! He *plagiarized* it. How could he have come up with my story? He's a narcissist. A *repressed* narcissist."

The bartender brought me my water. "He a friend of yours?" he asked, gesturing toward Portnoy.

"More of an acquaintance."

"Well he's been making an asshole of himself all evening."

I slid onto the stool next to Portnoy. Though he was facing away, Portnoy tensed noticeably, feeling my presence with a slight shudder, the way a criminal might suddenly feel the cold air of a cop.

"Hello, Alex."

The two girls relaxed as Portnoy took his shrill focus off them and turned around. "Well, well, well. If it isn't Mr. Philip Roth."

"How are you, Alex?"

The girls quickly moved to a table.

"Me? Oh I'm just *fine*." He forced out an ugly laugh and fished a packet of Camels out of his pocket. He shook out a cigarette and pointed it at me.

"No, thanks."

"Oh, that's right. Mr. Philip Roth doesn't *smoke*."

"I had some surgery. . . . Look, what are you doing here?"

"I was just about to ask you the same thing," said Portnoy, lighting his Camel and sucking it.

"Somebody called me. They said you were passed out in the men's room."

Portnoy shrugged. "I'm fine. As you can see." He began coughing and wiped his nose on his sleeve.

"You look like shit."

"Thanks. They called you, huh?"

"I was on my way to the theater."

"It's been thirty-five years, *you prick*."

"What?"

"Thirty-five years since publication, but there's been nothing. No Silver Anniversary edition. No film. No stage musical. Not even a book on tape."

"There *was* a film."

"Oh yeah, that. Richard Benjamin as me. Ridiculous. I don't even think he's Jewish. There should be a remake. Ed Norton would be good. Rob Lowe."

"I don't think Rob Lowe is Jewish."

Portnoy slammed his fist on the bar. "You don't *get* it, Roth, do you? I was an *icon*. I caught the Zeitgeist. I *was* the Zeitgeist."

"You want a musical?"

"Look at the *The Graduate*—it's on Broadway. *Hogan's Heroes* is a big movie. The Rolling Stones are on tour forever. If you *sneezed* in the sixties, they give you a miniseries. I'm nothing. Look at me— I'm pathetic."

I looked at my watch. I could feel Portnoy stealing a glance at it. So it's a Rolex. So what? "What do you want me to do about it, Alex?"

"Write a sequel. Joe Heller did. Vonnegut keeps bringing back Kilgore Trout—and *he's* an idiot, I can tell you. I went fishing with him once in Newfoundland. What an asshole. He kept stealing my worms, talking about some science fiction thing he'd written that was supressed by Vonnegut. Even Updike went back to Rabbit— another loser."

"Rabbit is dead."

"And he *still* got another book."

"You want a sequel?"

"I'm a great character!"

"I'm working on other things now, Alex."

"Don't make me beg."

"I've got my hands full with Zuckerman as it is. . . ."

"That narcissistic prick! Nobody likes him—he's completely full of himself. And talk about *pretentious*. Who'd ever want to be stuck in an elevator with Nathan Zuckerman? I'm funny. I'm pure id—and I've got a great libido. I'm fun! Do you realize how many letters I got?"

"You got letters?"

"Well, no. But only because nobody knew how to reach me. People stopped me on the street all the time. I'm desperate, man. You wouldn't want me to make a scene in public, would you?

"Just keep away from the college girls."

"Why, what's it to you? How about I expose myself in Washington Square Park? How'd you like *that* on Page Six? 'Roth Character Arrested on Morals Charge.' That'd make a nice little headline in the *Post*."

"Is that a threat?"

"I guess Zuckerman would never do a thing like that, huh? He goes to medical school. He's *intellectual*. You always liked him better."

"It's not a matter of 'like,' Alex. I just grew out of you, that's all. Why don't you give yourself a break and move up to Westchester? Or France?"

Portnoy laughed. "Portnoy in France, huh? How much of an idiot do you think I am? There aren't any Jews in France. Listen up, bub. If I don't get a sequel, I just might do something you'll live to regret."

"You're bluffing."

"Oh yeah?" He stood up and unzipped his pants.

The bartender held up his hands and motioned a time out. "Whoa, boys, that's it. . . ."

I grabbed Portnoy and muscled him outside. He squinted up at the streetlight.

"Get ahold of yourself, Alex. You can't act this way. And what are you doing in the Village? At the very least you should have gone to Elaine's."

"Are you kidding me? Everyone at Elaine's is about sixty years old."

"*You're* sixty years old!"

And here he punched me. It was a weak punch, catching me off the side of my jaw, but I wasn't expecting it. I was just about to sock him back when my cell phone began ringing. I took it out of my inside pocket and flipped it open.

"Hello?"

"Hello? Philip? It's Nathan."

Oh shit. "Zuckerman?"

Portnoy immediately perked up. "Perfect," he said dryly.

"Look, Nathan, this really isn't the best time. . . ."

"I wouldn't call you if it wasn't important, you know that. I know we've been kind of on the outs since you married a Communist."

"*I* married a Communist."

"Exactly. I got barely a walk-on. It was a like being in a Woody Allen film. One of the later ones."

"That's ridiculous."

Portnoy was straining to listen in. "What's he saying?"

I could hear the crackling coming over the cell line—a digital disassembling of spackled sound. "Nathan?"

"Yeah, I'm here. It's just that . . ." I heard a pointillist crash. "Carnovsky's here and I think he's wacked out on drugs."

"*Carnovsky?*" I said incredulously.

"Carnovsky?" echoed Portnoy. "That two-bit knockoff of *me*? Where is he?"

I put a hand over the phone. "Alex, please . . ."

"That guy's more pathetic than Trout. A fictional character of a fictional character. And *Zuckerman Unbound* is one of your weakest books. Everyone says so."

"Shut up, Alex." Then, into the phone: "Where are you, Nathan?"

"I'm, uh . . ." I heard another disembodied crash. "I don't know. I've been kind of floating around since my last cameo appearance. I have enough problems without having to deal with Carnovsky."

Portnoy pointed to the phone. "Tell him he had eight books and to shut the fuck up."

"Who's that?" said Zuckerman.

"I've got Portnoy here."

"Oh boy. What a night, huh?" Zuckerman laughed wistfully, and I remembered why I liked him so much. We had a lot in common, and now we were both dealing with unruly creations. I looked over and saw Portnoy urinating on a fire hydrant.

"Nathan, see if you can get Carnovsky over to Elaine's, okay?"

"How? What should I tell him?"

"Um . . . Tell him I miss him. That I'm thinking of writing a sequel to *Carnovsky*."

"I don't know if it'll work. You never really wrote *Carnovsky* in the first place. *I* wrote *Carnovsky*. Or at least, you claimed I did. But none of it was actually written."

"So tell him now I want to write it."

Portnoy was muttering in the background. He started singing drunkenly: *"Carnovsky is fartsky . . ."*

"What's that?" asked Zuckerman.

"Nothing. Just tell Carnovsky what I said and meet me at Elaine's in half an hour."

"I'll see what I can do."

In the taxi heading uptown, Portnoy was still drunkenly singing: *"Zuckerman-sham is a drunken man and Carnovsky is a cunt . . ."*

"Will you cut it out, Alex? I have a headache and I was supposed to be at dinner by now."

"Boo hoo hoo. Should've figured Zuckerman had your cell number."

"You really should hear how pathetic you sound. Jealousy isn't a very attractive trait."

"Sorry, Philip. You're right." He began tapping on the window as we passed Madison Square "I never congratulated you on getting the National Book Award for *American Pastoral*."

"Thanks. It was the Pulitzer Prize."

"Great. Why don't you shove it up your ass?"

I was not the first author to be confronted with the rebellion of his creations. Truman Capote once told me that Holly Golightly was constantly hitting him up for money, sometimes calling him in the middle of the night. She once pointedly threatened to crash the set of *Breakfast at Tiffany's* and physically assault Audrey Hepburn, whom she considered much too "goody-goody" for the role (Golightly, if she couldn't play it herself, would have preferred Edie Sedgwick for the part). And the primary reason Salinger became a recluse was that Holden Caulfield threatened to beat the shit out of him if he ever set foot in New York again. (He did once, to pick up a pair of Ferragamo shoes, and Caulfield tried to push him in front of a bus.)

But not even Tolstoy had ever had to confront so many unruly characters on a single evening.

When we arrived at Elaine's, I could hear a commotion at the back of the restaurant. Elaine Kaufman came over to us. "Who are you?"

"Elaine, it's me, Philip."

"Philip who?"

"Roth."

"Oh, sorry, I didn't recognize you. Thank God you're here— they're totally wrecking the place. George Plimpton tried to intercede, and Carnovsky hit him with a barstool. Mailer and Styron both got stabbed with a knife. I think the wounds were superficial, but I sent them to St. Vincent's anyway. Then I went for a—."

Portnoy grabbed Elaine and kissed her flush on the lips. She tried to push him away, but I could see it was pretty half-hearted. When he finally finished, she caught her breath and looked at me distractedly. "So who's your friend?"

"Never mind," I said. I went to the back of the restaurant where Zuckerman was trying to stop Carnovsky from setting fire to a table. There was no one else in the restaurant, but I could see from several overturned tables that a lot of diners had left in a hurry. As soon as they saw me they both stopped what they were doing.

"Kepish? Is that you?" Zuckerman said.

"No, it's Philip Roth," I said.

"That's impossible. Philip Roth died on an operating table ten years ago."

"No, it's me. You just called me."

"I don't remember that."

"You are Zuckerman, aren't you?"

"Me? No, I'm Philip Roth."

Carnovsky laughed.

"You just said he died ten years ago," I said.

"Of course I did. I can say whatever I like. I'm Philip Roth."

I stumbled into the men's room. It was pitch-dark. I found the light switch and turned it on. It was a small room with a single sink. I filled it with water and splashed some on my face. Then I stared at myself in the mirror. Who was I? Had I really died ten years ago? Was I someone else? Over the years I'd created so many alter egos for myself, how could I be sure who I was anymore? *Was I anyone?*

When I came out of the bathroom, the man I'd thought was Zuckerman was laughing. "Don't worry," he said. "I was just kidding you."

"Wow. Don't scare me like that." I laughed too.

"I'm not Philip Roth. Roth is in Tel Aviv at a Philip Roth convention. I'm Kepish."

The room started swirling. I sat down at an empty table. "So who am I?"

"You're Zuckerman."

I tried to get up but almost collapsed. "I have to go meet some . . . I have plans to . . ." I made my way back to the bar. Portnoy and Carnovsky were sitting next to each other, silently staring into each other's eyes. I couldn't help noticing that Carnovsky had his hand on Portnoy's leg and was stroking his thigh. Kepish came over to me and patted me on the back. "Turns out they're both fairies. Explains a lot, huh?"

I shrugged. What did it matter now, anyway? What was I even doing there? Where was I supposed to be? "Why didn't Roth invite us to the Roth convention? We did most of the work."

"Are you kidding? You know what a narcissist he is."

"I have to go," I said. "I'm supposed to have dinner with some friends."

"Which friends?"

I felt dizzy. "I . . . I don't know."

"It was us, Nathan. It was us all the time."

Elaine gestured to a table where a waiter had just set four places. Carnovsky and Portnoy, now holding hands, joined Kepish and me at the table. There was a lot to talk about. Volumes, in fact.

KURT VONNEGUT

GRADUATION SPEECH

Great scholars, weary professors, proud parents, jealous siblings: This is my new Graduation Speech. I apologize if it sounds generic. I've been using it all over the country. But in my defense, humans are by nature generic creatures—unlike the canowict fly of the west, a little dazzler if there ever was one.

More of him later. But let's get on to the Graduation Speech.

We assemble this afternoon, in this rented convention hall, to launch these young people like hopeful missiles upon an anxious world. We hope that they will explode into, as the bumper sticker has it, random acts of senseless kindness.

Yes, I just quoted a bumper sticker. We're at that stage where we grab at whatever makes a ha'penny of sense and throw it at the foe. Even bumper stickers, and what have you. It's a trick you learn as you get on in years. And I'm certainly that.

Each year is much like the last one, and none more so than the present *annus horribilus* in which we find ourselves today. The world is perched on the edge of a precipice—as it always is. Youngsters—many barely older than Charlie Brown and Lucy—are fighting old men's wars, as per usual. Good grief. Our fragile planet teeters on the edge of environmental collapse, as it has for a while. Picture it:

Little bunny rabbits rasping and spluttering as they try to breathe. (I put the image in Disney terms so you can see it. Most misery and suffering is invisible to the human eye.)

Winston Churchill—a great man who smoked cigars till the day he died at the unlikely age of ninety-one—famously told this to his listeners in the dire opening days of World War Number Two: "I have nothing to offer but blood, toil, tears and sweat." Imagine our current president saying something like that. Imagine anyone listening.

Imagine it.

Today I have nothing to offer you but a few hundred words of homilies and short sentences with a few colons.

For several years, a graduation speech—attributed to yours truly—circulated on the Internet. It was a document of superb sentiment and admirable brevity. But I didn't write it.

I entertained the notion of claiming authorship and reading that speech to you today. After all, ideas are free, and words of bravery and honesty should be circulated as freely as possible.

In fact, that non-Vonnegut speech can be accessed on the Internet for free. I urge you to seek it out at www.graduationspeech. com/notvonnegut_hll. If I had my own Web site, I'd probably urge you to visit that too. ("Visit." How quaint our notions of travel have become. But then, even old Henry Thoreau claimed he had traveled extensively . . . "in Concord." Yes, in Concord.)

But I don't have a Web site. There is no Vonnegut.com, because I have nothing more to say. I have banged my head on a hundred radiators, in cities across the world, and I've come up with nothing but a pallid collection of books in fancy dust jackets. Plus the memory of that eloquent bumper sticker.

Man has already been given a library card—and what has he done with it? What has *she* done with it? Nothing but left it on the bus. Personhood has massacred the innocents and belched coal dust into the sky.

Perhaps you'll do better. I look out and see your fresh-scrubbed faces, your mortarboards adorned with good-luck trinkets, and I see a rabble of startling youth, of vigor and beauty, with brains perhaps already poisoned by fashionable cynicism. Reject it. My own cynicism is certainly not fashionable, but accumulated over years of worry and regret.

You know better. You *are* better.

Well, I hope you are better. I hope you are vessels filled with naïveté and hope.

And so I launch these missiles of hope and wide-eyed enthusiasm into a lousy world wracked and exhausted by sheer neglect.

Your job is to fix everything.

Everything.

To make it all good again.

That's my speech. I dedicate it to the canowict fly, species number 9458625498. They don't have numbers, of course. I'm bestowing one of them for simplicity's sake. A canowict fly would as soon take a number as it would write a bumper sticker or set off a nuclear missile test in the Nevada desert. Even so, they're getting wiped out—by the millions. They're sensitive creatures—not like us. We can eat poisoned beef—meat polluted by our own Frankensteinian desire to create bigger and more perfect steaks—and even with our immune systems all shot to hell by the overuse of antibiotics, we can still live for years and years and years, doing unfathomable evil. We're freaks of nature, really. Gargoyles.

We Americans have an expression, said by someone who is supposedly absurdly pacific in nature: "He wouldn't hurt a fly." But of course we all hurt flies every day, whether we know it or not. And swatting them is the least of it.

The missile tests we set off in the Nevada desert half a century ago are killing the canowict fly. What did these insects do to us? I'll tell you what they did: absolutely nothing. If they had fur and were seen illustrated on chocolate Easter eggs, we might care. I'm calling Michael Eisner in the morning, urging him to make a hundred-million-dollar animated feature starring cute renditions of the canowict fly. Then something might happen.

Until then, you'll have to take my word for it that these are good, decent bugs, and not the quiet guys you might think, either. If you put a very sensitive microphone in front of their front legs and turned the sound way up, you'd hear their delectable mating

call, which goes something like this: "Arrrrrrrrrrrrrrrrrrrmmmm-
mmmmmmmmmmmmmmmmmmmmmmmpp!"

Pretty nifty, eh? Try putting that on a bumper sticker.

Well, that's my speech.

Yes, you have a lot of work to do.

So get cracking.

Thank you.

TERRY McMILLAN

WAITING TO INHALE

So it's Tuesday night which means Nombray Club. That's me and Gloria and Shoreen meeting at the Polo Lounge on Broadway at 115th for cocktails. "Nombray" because each one of us has "no hombre." Geddit? Stupid, I know, but we had to call it something, and we were sick of calling it Girls Night Out. We can't meet Sunday because that's *Sex and the City,* and Monday is *Ally McBeal,* so Tuesday is our club night and we can talk.

Anyway, so it's just the three of us, having kicked out Sophia and Shana. Anyone who gets a man gets kicked out of Nombray. We're very strict about that.

I was suspicious of Gloria from the start, because Shoreen and I were gabbing away about Ally's latest embarrassing screwup and Gloria was in another world. Something was definitely up.

"Gloria," I said finally. "Girl, I know you are hiding *something*. And I can see you are plainly *bursting* to tell us."

"Yeah," said Shoreen. "Who is he? Fess up!"

Gloria slunk low into her chair, and then this big grin comes on her face. She sits up straight as a rock. "Okay," she says. "Yeah, it's true. I met a guy."

"Well, obviously. What's he like?"

"Tall. Smart. Funny. Sensitive. Full of energy. Oh, and white."

"Get *out*," says Shoreen. "You're dating a white guy? Where'd you meet him?"

"Right here in Harlem."

"What is he? A cop?"

Gloria laughed. "Actually, he's out of work at the moment."

"Laid off? Or fired?" Shoreen had a look of satisfaction on her face as she took a sip of her Chardonnay.

"No, no, he's retired," said Gloria.

"Retired?" Now it was my turn to be skeptical. "How old is this guy? Seventy-three?"

Shoreen and I looked at each other and laughed, clinking our glasses.

"No, he's in his fifties, actually. But they made him retire. It doesn't matter, I mean, the man has *money*. But that's not why I like him. He's sensitive. And for a white guy he's pretty black. He says he feels my pain, and I believe him."

"Why, do you kick him in the head? 'If you can't stand the skeet . . .'"

"Get out of the kitchen!" Shoreen and I say in unison. And we fall into peals of laughter.

Gloria is not amused. "Hardy-har. Let's just say, for a white guy, he knows what he's doing." And now it was her turn to hold up her glass and, with a knowing look, drink to us. Shoreen and I fell silent.

I don't need to tell you, I was curious. Gloria said she'd met Bill at the Starbucks on 125th Street, and damn if I didn't start hanging out there after work at Mess. I'm a senior account exec at Messner Vetere Berger MacNamee Schmetterer RSCG. We used to make jokes about the name all the time. "Is that your business card or are you just happy to see me?" That was one of them. I used to feel sorry for the receptionists, because they weren't allowed to abbreviate the name, so every three seconds they have to answer the phone: "Messner Vetere Berger MacNamee Schmetterer RSCG—may I help you?" But it's how *I* started out, so fuck them. Gotta start somewhere.

Mess is way downtown in what I call WoHo (West SoHo), so I

have about a thirty-five-minute commute from my apartment on 135th Street. Usually I read the latest Toni or maybe *O Magazine* (which is okay, though I'm waiting for Oprah to get off the damn cover). But lately I've had my mind elsewhere. I've been thinking about Gloria's Big Bad Bill.

He's a real homebody, apparently, only it's never *his* home. He likes to stay in and watch movies or sports on TV. And boy can he *talk*. Gloria says he can talk knowledgeably on just about anything—global politics, free trade, the Harlem Renaissance, Jordan's latest comeback, books, films, music—you name it. And boy can he *eat*. "He is passionate about everything," says Gloria. "Especially food and sex."

Well, that got me going. Food and sex are about my two favorite things in the world. I tell you, I would have hunted him down and called him up myself, but Gloria is a friend of mine and I don't poach.

But if I happened to run into him at Starbucks, that's something else. He never showed, though. Gloria said he'd been traveling lately and she hadn't heard from him in a couple of weeks. She assumed it was over.

Then one night, as I was about to get into bed, the phone rang.

"Hello, Jeannie?" It was a horse voice, like the guy was just getting over a cold or something. Maybe he'd been shouting at someone.

"Who's this?" I asked.

"This is Bill. You know, Gloria's friend."

Bill. Well, *hello,* Bill. "Uh huh?" I said.

"Gloria told me a bit about you. She got me real curious." The guy sounded southern, for chrissake. Generally, I don't go for southern white guys.

"What'd she say about me?"

"Oh, just that you were smart and sexy and liked to have a good time."

"Really? That doesn't sound like Gloria."

"Okay, you got me. I confess: I interpolated that from other stuff she said."

"That sounds more likely."

"So I was just sitting up here in my lonely house in Westchester and thought I'd call you up."

"Uh-huh . . ."

"Thought maybe you'd come out and have some fun."

I didn't say anything for a moment. Just let the thought hang there for a while.

"Gloria?"

"I'm here, Bill. What kind of fun did you have in mind?"

"Oh, you know—thought I might drive down there. You live in Harlem, right? Thought we could get ourselves some wings, maybe take them back to your place. Have you ever seen *To Kill a Mockingbird?* It's a great film. I got it on tape."

"What's wrong with your place?"

There was a pause.

"My house is kind of a mess at the moment."

"Aren't you married, Bill?"

"Only in the loosest technical sense."

I noticed the spiral cord on my phone was wound twice around my right index finger—a habit of mine when I'm feeling a bit anxious. It's why I can't quite bring myself to get a cordless phone. A girl needs all the thermometers she can get.

"What about Gloria?" I said.

And here I heard a friendly, good-natured chuckle. "Gloria is a very lovely lady."

I was expecting more, but he left it at that. Despite myself, I was impressed by his boldness. And he could tell I was interested.

"Jeannie? The night isn't getting any longer."

Okay, that ticked me off a bit, and for the first time I found him a little pushy. I was still interested—but I wanted to force him into the open.

"You know a place called the Victoria Lounge?"

"A bar?" he said skeptically.

"It's a cocktail lounge. Don't worry, no one ever goes there."

When I got to Victoria, the place was packed—as I knew it would be. I looked all around the bar and couldn't see him—or what I assumed he would look like. For a moment I thought the bastard had stood me up!

"Hey, Jeannie . . ." It was a hoarse stage whisper. "Yo, Jeannie—here . . ."

He was sitting at a booth in the back, in the dark. I could just make out a strong jaw and some unruly gray-white hair.

"Bill?"

He half-stood as we shook hands, him grabbing my elbow with his other hand in one of those Israeli-Palestinian peace armshakes that have questionable results. "So glad you could come."

He had a warm presence, and he was much bigger than I expected—bigger in the sense of *substantial*. The man had *gravitas*. But he also look exhausted—the rings under his eyes practically had box seats.

"What can I get you to drink? Red wine? Cosmopolitan?"

"A red wine would be nice."

He waved a hand and instantly a young woman in a tiny black dress materialized before us: a mocha-skinned twenty-one-year-old model-waitress type with a toothy smile that could have jump-started a stalled tank.

"Hello, Sugar," he purred. "A red wine for the lovely lady here." Bill managed to look like a CEO and talk like a pimp, flirting with the waitress at the same time he was complimenting me and I thought, *Uh-oh, Sister, this one's a player.*

But still, the man had style. He was wearing a light gray suit that looked Brooks Brothers or Bergdorf's, and even though we were sitting in the back, out of the way, you could tell he still felt as if he owned the place, as if he was used to commanding whatever situation he was in. He gazed around at the groups of chatting and gesticulating yuppies and buppies, and chuckled as if bemused by his surroundings.

"This place is more crowded than I was expecting."

"It's odd," I said. "It's usually dead on a weeknight."

He knew I was fibbing, and he knew I knew he knew, which just had the effect of bringing us closer together, two conspirators sussing each other out.

Then he turned to me and blatantly looked me over. "You sure look nice. How come we never met before?"

"I guess we've both been busy."

"I'll say." He continued looking at me, but now at my face, staring into my eyes. "Seriously," he said. "How you doing?"

"I'm okay."

"Really?" He looked tired, but also looked used to being tired, and used to not letting it get in the way of his concern for others. It was very appealing. He began asking me about my job, my family, my loves and longings. To be honest, he got a lot out of me—he had this incredibly insidious empathy. It was like unloading to a psychiatrist, though infinitely more comforting (and cheaper). I felt my defenses beginning to wane. I'd come intending to be distant and mysterious, to sip a single glass of Chardonnay and smile at him enigmatically, and when I left—after less than an hour—I'd leave him dangling and confused.

But I was the one who was confused, unloading about the various men who had betrayed me and screwed me over, how all I just wanted to be was *married*.

"I'm really surprised," he said. "A lovely lady like you shoulda been snatched a long time ago."

Snatched? I suddenly remembered his own matrimonial status.

"As a rule, you know, I don't go out with married men."

"Me too." He smiled.

It was a stupid joke, but I laughed. Bill had an uncanny ability to make me feel at ease, and within minutes I felt that we'd been friends for years. I also felt that he wanted to be more than friends. And fast.

My wine arrived, placed on the table by the little Halle Berry flashing a surly glance at me, and a quick, furtive (though I saw it all right) smile at Bill. He pretended not to notice it. He told me he liked New York, especially Harlem, where he had an office, but that he had too much time on his hands. He used to live in Washington, but he was glad to have left. "That place is full of back-stabbing, lying sonsabitches and incompetent retards." His wife still lived there and his daughter had moved to California. He was all alone now.

Poor chile. Yeah, he was laying it on a bit thick, I thought, overplaying his hand. The music was already making me kind of nauseous when Kenny G came on the sound system and I was about to make a crack, when I noticed Bill's right hand drumming on the table along to the music. His left hand was on my knee.

We took a cab to my place (okay, so rules are made to be broken). Gloria was right about his bedroom abilities—I'd give him *magna cum laude*. He was considerate, adventurous—and enduring. His only quirk was that he insisted on having the TV on and tuned to C-Span throughout the whole thing, which I found a bit off-putting at first. The Senate was debating a farm bill, by the sound of it, with various politicians droning on about taxes and subsidies. But after a while I began to enjoy the perversity of it, and I came— loud and clear (*magna come louder*)—just as Tom Daschle was making some kind of point of order.

I'd hardly caught my breath when Bill was up and running again, but by the time he'd reached for the condom, he'd wilted. I glanced over at the TV and saw that the junior senator from New York was monotoning a speech. Bill reached for the remote and quickly turned off the set.

"Sorry, Hon. Lost my concentration."

"Hey, don't worry about it." I was looking for a cigarette. "Happens to the best of 'em."

"No, really, it doesn't happen much to me." He was staring vaguely at the silenced television and looked momentarily lost.

I reached over to the side table and pulled open the drawer, rifling through the tissues and nail files and emergency Trojans till I felt the small paper sliver I was searching for. I found a lighter too and lit the joint. Bill watched me warily as I took a deep toke and handed the joint to him.

"No, thanks."

"Go on," I said. "Do you some good."

He studied the joint pinched in his fingers and then waved it affably, like a cigarette. "Hell, I'm not working. What the hell. This is my *holiday*." And with that he brought the joint to his mouth and took the longest drag I'd ever seen. I thought for sure he'd pass out, but he finally exhaled—a cloud of smoke that momentarily buried his head in a silver cloud. And then the laughter—peals and peals of laughter—and his face suddenly turned boyish and seemed to change its pallor, so much so that the rings around his now-bloodshot eyes seemed to disappear.

The rest of the night I just lay in his arms, in the middle of his huge bear embrace, and we talked and talked until the sun came up. And it felt like I was in the safest, warmest place on earth.

The next day I called Shoreen to resign my membership in the Nombray Club. We'd already kicked out Gloria for her Bill assignations. But now that he was mine, I figured Shoreen could take Gloria back in the club, and I was on the outs.

"It's funny," Shoreen said. "I was just about to call you. I'm out of the club too."

"You been dating? Who is the poor bastard?" I laughed.

"You know that guy Gloria was talking about? Bill?"

I didn't say anything.

"He called me up the other day. We've been, kind of, getting it together."

"No, really, Shoreen. Who is it?"

"Why? He isn't still seeing her. Is he?"

I looked down at the roach in the ashtray and thought about the night before.

"You know, Shoreen," I said. "I think it's time to disband the Nombray Club. How about next week we all just go to the movies?"

FRANK McCOURT

ANGELA'S EYELASHES

When I look back on my childhood I wonder how I still have my own teeth. Dental hygiene was not exactly foremost in the thoughts of the poor of Limerick, Ireland, but you'd think I might have found a toothbrush somewhere, or even run a thread of catgut along the incisors.

It was, of course, a poetic childhood. A prosaic childhood is hardly worth your while. Worse than a poetic childhood is an Irish poetic childhood. And worse than a poetic Irish childhood is a poetic Irish Catholic childhood without a toothbrush. Any odd penny I found went to a piece of toffee or chocolate. My dad didn't want me to brush my teeth. He wanted me to be champion of all pint drinkers.

I'm ten when he first takes me down to the pub to watch him riverdance for pints. He's a regular lord of the dance, says the barman, who has to speak in a high-pitched French accent on account of being gassed in the war.

Champion of all pint drinkers, says Donny O'Donnel.

But there are only so many riverdances the drinkers of Limerick can take from a drinker with the sneaky air of a northern Presbyterian, so Dad is forced to sell my brother Malarky and me to a local farmer as wheelbarrows. We spend eight hours a day being rolled about the dank countryside, covered in shit. The farmer's wife likes the look of Malarky, all blond and smiling. What a pretty wheelbarrow, she says.

One day Mam must notice that we're missing because she tracks us down to the farm and takes us home. But there's no money to buy coal, and it's so cold at night Malarky and I have to pee on each other to keep warm. We call it the Limerick Fire. I pee on Malarky, and Malarky pees on the twins and the twins pee on the baby. The baby then sits on Mam and pisses all over her, which gets her up.

What's this? she cries out.

It's the Limerick Fire, says Malarky.

One of the twins is crying. Frankie won't piss on me, he says.

Francis McCourt, what's the world coming to if you won't piss on your little brother?

I peed on him yesterday, I say.

Francis McCourt, it's a fine way to treat your little brother who never did you an inch of harm in your life. Now go over there and piss on his head.

I'm all out, I tell her. I'm done pissing. I need to drink some more tea. But there's no more tea, and not a crumb to eat in the house. The baby is crying again, so we all take turns spitting in his bottle and we mix it with some dirt from the lane. The baby takes the bottle and this quiets him down for a while.

Malarky is turning gray. He has diphtheria, TB, and the Demented Sheep Disease. Lord knows how he got the Demented Sheep Disease because we haven't had lamb in donkey's years. Or even donkey, for that matter.

We all try to go back to sleep, lying under our flea-ridden coats. Thank God it's Friday and Dad will be home soon with the dole money. But it's after midnight and there's no sign of him.

Then we can hear him singing loudly down in the lane.

> *Oh England has enslaved us going on 800 year*
> *Killing our dreams and instilling us with fear*
> *But Erin will wake from her long-time sleep*

As sure as Shannon runs so cold and deep
I sing to the Lord and the good Cuchulain
And sorry I drunk all the dole money again

He calls from the bottom of the stairs, Angela, Angela, is there a drop of tea in the house?

Mam refuses to answer him in this state.

Dad comes upstairs, stinking of beer, and gets me and Malarky up.

Will you get drunk for Ireland, lads?

Yes, we say sleepily.

Yes, what?

Yes, sir.

No no, says Dad. I mean, what will you do?

Get drunk, we say.

Get drunk for what? asks Dad.

Get drunk for Ireland, we say.

Good lads. Here's your Friday penny. And he handed us each a little stone.

What's this, Dad? A stone?

Oh aye, there are people who would give their right nipples for a stone. Or even a pebble.

We're so hungry, Malarky and I, that we eat the stones in a single gulp.

Michael has dragged home another dead dog and we toss it in the pot with some worms and bird droppings. It's like Christmas, it is, with dead dog and roasted sweet pigeon for dessert. The rich people of Derringdong Street can have their goose and drink their tea with their little fingers out. We've got dead dog and pigeon. We give the eyeballs to Mam.

No, give Francis the eyeballs she says, he needs them to strengthen his eyes, Lord help me.

I don't much like the look of the eyeballs, staring up at me from the dog soup, but I scoop one of them out and bite into it. It tastes like chicken. Malarky with his TB and Demented Sheep Disease stares at me hungrily, so I give him the other eyeball. He swallows it in a single gulp, and it gets stuck in his throat. He's honking and making odd sounds. Finally I take a stick and bash him on the head. The eye goes shooting out of his mouth and sticks on the far wall.

Mrs. O'Yenta comes by and she and Mam sit downstairs smoking Woodbangs.

Oh, I'm a martyr to the fags, says Mam.

Mrs. O'Yenta says, Did you hear what happened to Dolly O'Dea's son Wigen O'Wye?

No what?

Got hit by a motor car standing in the middle of Rosbrien Road, he did. Knocked him stone dead.

Isn't he the lucky one? What I wouldn't do to be run over by a motor car.

And 'tis true, in Limerick the best thing that can happen to you is to be run over by a motor car. I go out to Rosbrien Road and stand in the middle of the street for three days, but there's a not a single car that runs me over. Get out of the street, you damn eejit, yells a driver, swerving around me.

I come home and find the downstairs flooded again. Mam is upstairs with Mrs. O'Yenta. What's wrong with Francis's eyes? she says.

They're mangy, says Mam.

Sure there's a cure for that. You need a stick.

A stick, you say?

A sharp-pointed stick. You jam it in his eyes, to let the goo out.

I'm thinking this doesn't sound so good, a stick in my eyes.

Sheila O'Donlanfan's son Paddy had sick eyes. They poured hot wax on his head and set fire to his feet. Now he sees as well as a cat from the Day of the Assumption to the Feast of the Circumcision.

Does he now, says Mam.

Either that or you can rub his eyes with rotten grapes.

After Mrs. O'Yenta leaves, Mam says, Rotten grapes, is it? And where would she have us find grapes in Limerick, rotten or no. Rotten apples is more like it. No, we'll have to poke your eyes, and then the hot wax and the burnt feet.

• • •

After Mam has poked my eyes and poured hot wax on my head and set fire to my feet, I'm in the hospital. They say I have malaria, Spanish Lung, and Indonesian Crazed Monkey Disease. All the wards are full up with the recent outbreak of Sorry Water, so they put me down in the morgue lounge, which is very noisy during visiting hours with families crying for their deceased relatives. But it's also next to the hospital library, and I spend my days reading the complete works of Shakespeare and Dickens and Mark Twain. I'm also fed regularly and it's so warm that after a couple of weeks I stop asking the nurses to pee on me.

Mam visits me whenever she can, but it's a six-mile walk from Ratbog Lane and by the time she arrives it's usually after visiting hours, so she has to shout to me from the street. She tells me that Dad has gone to Scotland to build bagpipes for the war effort, and Malarky has joined an army dance team in Dublin.

After six weeks the nurses tell me I'm well enough to return home. I'm not looking forward to leaving the food and books, and as I walk home I think about how I've changed. Reading Evelyn Waugh and P. G. Wodehouse and Wisden's *Cricketers Almanack* has given me a new outlook on life.

The house looks smaller than I remember it, and I mount the stairs with a certain amount of trepidation.

I see Mam sitting on the crate, smoking a Woodbang. Don't you look grand.

Tally ho, Mater, I say.

I notice she has a new baby at each breast. The twins died, she says. But these arrived on the seventh step.

So it's no net loss, I observe.

What?

You look different, Mater. Pray tell, what changes have been afoot your face?

A foot on my face?

No, I mean—

I sold my eyelashes, she says. Your father drinks his money in Scotland and there's nothing coming in. There are rich English women born with no eyelashes and they pay good money for them.

That was the beginning of the end of my life in Limerick. With

Mam's eyelashes gone and everyone in the lane failing to understand my new augmented vocabulary, I knew it was time to go to
America.

There, in the land of freedom and promise I worked as a high
school teacher in the South Bronx for the next forty-two years. It
was a tough life. But I never had to sell my eyelashes.

DON DeLILLO

AMERICAN OPENER

They march softly, uniformed blue, pushing canvas bags on wheels, up driveways, through garden gates, the ceaseless march of delivery, past anonymous rubble and manicured lawns, over driveways of pampered asphalt warm to the touch. Like ghost soldiers they slip their paper cache through brass slits and into tin canisters of horizontal urgency, phallic torpedoes of American mail. Neither wind nor snow nor gloom of night shall stay these couriers from their appointed tasks.

The radio announces the third terrorist alert this week, this one a 3.2 (bridges, tunnels, airports, plus a possible airborne toxic event). We decide to stay home.

I don't trust the mailman. He shows up at odd times, looks distracted and otherwise engaged.

The government alerts are ridiculed now, tolerated with the ersatz respect accorded community theater. The president is the postmaster general, the head mail man playing Stanley Kowalski, reading his lines fitfully off cue cards. He walks with theatrical purpose, his arms away from his hips, fists clenched, like Popeye. *I yam what I yam.*

Who are these mailmen, and where do they come from?

The business-improvement district has been sealed off. Information is sketchy. Rumors are traded like hard currency, the new coin of the realm. An outside agitator got in (or an inside agitator got out). Crop dusters flew low over the city, spreading invisible contaminants. A mysterious package was found at the bus depot. Midgets posing as children have infiltrated the school system, their multicolor backpacks filled with plastic explosives.

We filter our water, we irradiate our mail. We scrub ourselves with detox powder and antibacterial soap. We wear face masks when we leave the house. How far away are radiation suits? Soon we will be Moonmen on Earth, visitors to our own planet.

And still they come—sweepstakes and magazines, postcards and bills. Every one a winner. You may have already won. This could be you.

What could be you? When you have won, you are no longer you.

And what could you win?

I look at the pile of mail on the inside mat with dread and distrust. I know that from benign letters unfurl a mysterious contagion, envelopes deliver dissonant air, the invisible ghost snow of distortion.

And still the mailmen march under the sulfurous wattage of a low shimmering sky, unsmiling, relentless, unstoppable.

Mono, my wife, looks out the picture window and sees the mailman approach. "He has on his shorts again."

"Embarrassing blue," I say, not looking.

"Don't ever wear anything like that."

"They're our occupying army, a national militia, the tenuous glue of democracy. Worker ants of ceaseless spirit, secular foot soldiers of paper product—"

"Did you pay the electricity bill?"

"Why?"

"Without electricity we freeze. We starve. We live in lightless gloom, reverting to the primal state, the Ground Zero of Year One."

"Soon there will be no more paper. But the mailmen will keep coming, pushing air through letter boxes, ringing doorbells for

nothing. Priests from the former age, the paper period. Like Bene-
dictine monks seeking alms."

"We'll have to tip them just to go away."

"So did you pay the electricity bill or not?"

"Wait. Which one are you? The husband or the wife? I can't
remember."

"Neither can I. We sound exactly the same."

We've turned the basement into a fallout shelter, the walls are lined
with Campbell's condensed soups—red-and-white cans of Pop Art
cuisine. Everything in the post-fallout world will be condensed—
we will read the classics in *Reader's Digest* editions, we will watch
edited sports highlights, and montage films like *That's Entertainment*
and *That's Entertainment Part 2.* Our music will be condensed——
greatest-hits collections, *Masters of the Baroque, Music to Eat To. Music
to Listen to Music To.*

But Mono has lost the can opener. In the half-life of the after-
world, how will we eat? The cans remain on metal shelves, virginal,
vacuum-packed, tantalizingly beyond use.

Mono has decorated the shelter like a Cold War den, with
framed photos of Eisenhower and Krushchev (the nemeses of Iron
Curtain chess), plus track lighting, a combination TV/hi-fi player
in a simulated walnut grain cabinet, and emergency Hoola-Hoops
in fire-engine red. Tom Lehrer is our poet laureate, Allen Ginsberg
is our beatnik saint. We watch eight-millimeter silent blue movies
of Betty Page smiling while being spanked in her black girdle and
leopard-print bra.

We feel more comfortable in the warm hum of the Cold War.
We listen regularly to the Emergency Broadcast System, saluting its
demonstrative squeal.

"Did you find the can opener yet?"

"No. I've looked everywhere."

"Did you look in the larder? Did you try the garret? Did you
peruse the utility room? Did you check the hacking jacket? What's
a hacking jacket?"

"The mailman is here again."

"Again? He was just here yesterday."

"He has a package for us, wrapped in noncommittal, proletarian, utilitarian brown."

"Mailed to you in a discreet, unmarked brown package, like Exuberant Breast Aficionado, or Olympian Leg Enthusiast."

"Surely pornography employs less pretentious titles than that."

"It's pornography for professors."

"And pretentious novelists."

The package turns out to be our new respirators. We test them in the backyard, venturing out as far as the gazebo, next to the satellite dish, in front of the barbecue grill. In our masks we look like huge insects, mutant beings of the post–Industrial Age. In the technological revolution, information was supposed to be the new economy, benign ones and zeros sent shooting through the bloodstream of the World Wide Web. But the Internet was the God that failed. Broadband wires pulse with poisoned light, hosting parasites of hard-drive destruction. The virus is in the mail.

"Did you find the can opener?"

"I'm still looking."

"From now on we get only pull-tab cans."

"Okay. From now on."

Mono wipes on a picture window a porthole view with her hand, rubbing away the dust. We stare out at the sulfurous sunset, a blot of neon colors in glassy air.

"It's as beautiful as a Toyota Celica."

"As beautiful, yes."

"It's a Toyota Celica sunset."

"Toyota Celica should be used more as a descriptive adjective."

"I agree with you."

We go into the kitchen and make some waffles. It's the most American thing we can think of, and we feel safer for it. Every little bit counts.

IRVINE WELSH

TRAINSPITTING

So it's a pisspot day and I'm fuckin sittin on my dank mog in the park, freezin off my fuckin tod, waitin for that skank geezer Skep to show his fuckin arsehole face, the shite cunt.

The birds are making a fuckin racket, all twee-twoo.

—SHUT IT YER FUCKIN SKANK BIRDS!

But then I'm lookin at the ducks, all a fambling on the great sick grey of the Serpentine scuzz and I'm thinkin: thems is roight fuckin genius birds they are, swimmin, walkin and like flyin, fer chrissake.

I'm in one roight fuckin philosophical mood.

Finally Skep shews his fat ugly gob, his ears budded into a skank walkman, and dried sick all over his mac.

—Ello Kep.

—Ello Skep, I say. Wots with the sick?

Skep looks down at his nasty coat and sniffs it.

—Not mine, he says.

—Wots on the buds?

—Iggy.

—Sick of the fuckin Ig.

—Don't knock the Ig if you don't want a roight bashin, yer dumbfock.

—Where's Smike?

—Fuckin trainspitting, he is.

—Wots trainspitting? I say, ripping the buds out of his ears.

—Geezer goes on a bridge, waits for the 4:10 from Reading. Drops a roight gob on the engine, like.

—Wotsit for?

—For nothin, says Skep. For a laugh. Somethin to do, ennit.

I give it a small think.—Fuckin stupid, that is. I prefer bus-fuckin. You ain't had a fuck till you've fucked a bus.

—For the birds, is bus-fuckin, Skep says. I used to bus-fuck, when I was a roight arsehole. Now I spikejam.

—Wozat?

—Take a rusty spike and jam it up yer arse. It's a roight comment on the plight of jobless youth. We're like the Spikejamming Generation.

—Yer off yer fuckin Churchill, I tell him. We're the Bus-fuckin Generation. Seen it on the telly.

—Well we're bloody well not the Trainspitting Generation. If I had to trainspit, I'd be better off smashing me head in.

—Oh yeh, Digby done that, I say.

—Done what?

—Done smashed his face in. Said it was the best thing he ever done. Now he got 96 stitches in his head. Looks like a bloody suitcase.

—Ha ha.

—Yeh, ha ha.

We shoff down to Buckingham Palace and Skep unzips and starts wheeing on the gates, all the while singing the national anthem.—*God save the fuckin queen, long fuck her skanky dream, god fuck James Dean . . .*

He zips up.—Always think of her fuckin majesty when I wizz. Gives my jizz an imperial knock.

And its true: the skank piss on the royal gates does have a roight fuckin majesty to it.

—ARGHHHHHHH! says Skep.

—Wo' izzit?

—Sorry. Got me cocker jammed in the zip.

—Ow.

We're watchin the wind-up loo brushes marching to and fro in the queen's front yard.

—Bloody great pillocks, says Skep. GET A REAL JOB YER FUCKIN SHITE CUNTS!

—Go easy, matey, I say. It's the queen's birthday. She's been on the royal crapper for 50 years.

And sayin it I realise what a patriotic fuck I am, and I felt a little rumbling in my nethers, my cocker rising in a royal salute. And suddenly the whole bleedin pageantry of the surroundings, the palace and the gates and the toilet brushes and the big fuckin statue of that fat arse Victoria conspire to give be a big fuckin hard-on. So I go over to the statue, unbutton and begin givin a grind to the edge of the statue—but in my head I'm giving a quick one to old Vicki, her black dress pushed up around her blubby hips, her enormous knickers pulled down, her fat thighs wrapped around my spotty arse.—Oh yeh, Vicki—Oh Vicki, that's great. Just lie back and think of England, you great fat cow, ooh yeh . . .

—Oy!

I look down to see a copper giving me the once over.

—Get down from there!

I quickly pull up me trousers and rabbit it up the Mall, where I find Skep pissing in the middle of the fuckin street, taxis swerving around him. He's like a fuckin dog, is Skep, whizzing all over the city, marking his fuckin territory.

—Yo, Skep. Where you going?

Skep shakes off and zips up—carefully this time.

—Got an errand, he says.

—You signing on then?

—Nah. Don't like to encourage the bastards. Just go down to the Savoy and nick luggage from bloody tourists. Then I fence it down in Peckham. It's a fuckin tough life, but it's a livin, you know?

—I just sign on.

—Coz yer a lazy cunt bastard.

Just then we see Spizz.

—Got any dosh?

—Nah.

Spizz looks like fillet of crap, his blue plastic parka all scraped and fucked.

—Wot happened to you? I ask him.

He looks at me in a daze.—Fell off the back of a truck.

So it's the three of us now, fuckin musketeers lookin to do some damage. There's no luggage at the Savoy because it's too early and even the sandwich shops are closed. So we go over to Trafalgar Square and start throwing each other in the fountains.

—Let's visit McHamish McMacMcMee.

—I bloody hate him, the Scotch cunt.

—Wots wrong with McMac?

—Bloody Scotch bastard, can't understand a word he says. Can't even pronounce his fuckin *name*.

—You just got to pay attention, you spunk fuck.

—I heard McMac had a fuckin ruckus in a pub, he did. Knocked a punter.

—Wot? I say.

—Shucked a duff cunt in a rigger.

—*Wot?*

—Had intercourse with a lady of dubious vintage in a down-market saloon.

—Oh, roight. Thought you meant he'd wagged a shit off a fagger in a plop.

—Eh? says Skep.

—Dug a bunghole in a cunt jag.

—Huh?

—Had rear-entry sexual relations with a woman in a toilet, only to later discover—much to his chagrin—that he had penetrated a man.

—Oh, roight. Fuckin hate it when that happens.

—Let's go jam some H in our arms, says Spizz.

—Great. I'm up in the pits, yeh.

We walk the seven miles down to Barnstead to visit McHamish McMacMcMee. When we get to his shed, McMac is covered in blood, hanging upside down by a light fixture, his legs tied with electrical cord. His mud-colored mutt is yapping and trying to nip at his feet.

—Is he dead? I ask Skep.

—Nah, that's how he sleeps. WAKE UP, MCMAC, YER GREAT PILLOCK!

We untie him and let him fall to the cement floor, which wakes him up.

—Wot mchappened? he says.

—Had a good sleep?

—Wisnae oan aboot, hudnae wank aboot off?

—Wot?

—Aye-o-aye, offnae oot nae eye.

—Um . . .

—Didnae scrip nae un oon nanny?

—Uh . . .

—Yer shed pres speck?

—Er . . . Maybe.

—Dis bin don der fock der nanny?

—Um . . .

—Der fock DER NANNY?

—No no, left der nanny alone.

McMacMcMee looks puzzled, as if a huge bird has just shat on his head. Which I notice it has.

—Fock—a bird done shat me mcnog!

McMac takes out a small vial of black liquid which he says is Euthenate, a mixture of the horse tranquilizer Derbithal and Vermint, a mouse poisoner with a minty aftertaste.

—Sounds great, I say. Give me some. How'd you take it?

—Inject it in your eyeballs, says Skep.

—Smashing.

So we're shooting Euthenate into our pupils and we decide to do the dog too. In a moment I find myself stapled to the floor, my fingernails dripping through the cracks in the floorboards, my stomach full of cinderblock. I fall asleep for several hours (minutes? days?) and I wake up to find my face in the dog's arse, lickin his bung. What am I doing lickin the bleedin dog? Then I realise it's my own arsehole—which it suddenly occurs to me isn't anatomically possible. I've turned into the ruddy dog!

Skep's turned into a sodding great aardvark, his tongue slithering out of his mouth like a snake.

—Whaz goin on, mate? I say. Only it comes out like this: OoooooooOhooo-yoooOOOOoooooHHH!!!

And then my tongue falls off, and I'm tumblin through a viscous space, swimmin in the thick marshlands of the Florida Keys.

I wake up in motion, yeah I'm flying through the trees about 15 feet off the ground. I look over to see Skep and Spizz passed out on red-plaid couches. We're on a bus upstairs, coasting through outer London. Streathem, by the look of it, the little sweet shops and pubs whizzing by.

—Oy, Skep. Oy, wake up. We're on a bus.

Skep comes to.—Where are we?

—On a fuckin bus.

—Bollocks.

But he looks out the window and sees.—Bloody 'ell. Better ge' off.

We stumble downstairs and jump off the back of the bus. It's not Streathem at all, but West Wickham.

—What now? says Spizz.

I look around and see the railway bridge.—Oy. Let's go trainspitting.

—Great, says Skep. Trainspitting it is then.

So like we head for the railway bridge. Well, somethin to do, ennit?

JONATHAN FRANZEN

ON OPRAH

This is a transcript of Jonathan Franzen's appearance on the Oprah Winfrey Show *that never aired. Franzen's celebrated novel* The Conniptions *had just been published.*

OPRAH: I'm very happy to have on my show a young writer of immense talent and ambition, whose new novel, *The Conniptions*, is now in stores. Please welcome . . . Jonathan Franzen.
(Applause)
FRANZEN *(from off set)*: I'm not doing it.
OPRAH: What?
FRANZEN *(off set)*: I'm not appearing on your show. I thought the driver was taking me to Charlie Rose, but it turned out to be *Oprah*. I'm staying in the Green Room. My book is firmly in the high-art tradition. My biggest fear, if I were to get the Oprah Seal of Approval, is that women might start reading my book. And I don't really see women as being in the high-art tradition.
OPRAH: Well, come on out so we can at least talk about it.
(Long pause.)
FRANZEN *(off set)*: Okay. But I'm not comfortable doing it.
(Jonathan Franzen comes out on stage, to muted applause. He sits in a large easy chair opposite Oprah.)

OPRAH: Welcome. I don't care what anyone says, including you—I love your book.

FRANZEN: Thank you, I guess.

OPRAH: You don't like doing TV?

FRANZEN: Not really. I don't even *have* a TV.

OPRAH: You don't?

FRANZEN: No. I have to watch the one in the apartment across the street, and he's usually watching game shows. And it's really hard to follow without the sound.

OPRAH: That reminds me of a funny story Whitney Houston once told me—

FRANZEN: There's a devaluation of adults in today's society, in which too much cultural product is aimed at children—or what I like to call "unadults." Too many books are written for these unadults.

OPRAH: Like what?

FRANZEN: Well, you've picked some of these pretty schmaltzy, one-dimensional, clitoral books, and frankly they make me cringe.

OPRAH: Clitoral?

Franzen: Maybe *vulvan* is a better term. *Mammarial?*

(He makes a note.)

OPRAH: You worked on this book for a long time.

FRANZEN: I spent six years writing this book, and three of those years were spent in an isolation tank, with my ears plugged, my nose blocked, my eyes covered, and my penis stuck into a catheter. You really can't get the right feel of a dysfunctional family at Christmas until you pee into a tube. I imagine that's how Joyce wrote the last part of *Ulysses.*

OPRAH: So you don't get out much.

FRANZEN: I never get out. I spent the eighties living in the basement of a burnt-out building in the South Bronx with my then-wife. We had no money. We'd get up at 4:00 A.M., write for twelve hours, break for lunch (Saltine crackers and curdled milk), then read for eleven hours, break for dinner (toasted raisins and hot water), and then write for another nine hours. We'd usually get to bed around 6 A.M.—and then start the whole thing again in the morning, often getting up two hours before we'd even gone to bed.

OPRAH: Wow.

FRANZEN: We went out only once a year, on our wedding anniversary.

OPRAH: Where would you go?

FRANZEN: We'd go to McDonald's and have two orders of McNuggets, no beverage. We'd bring our own water. We'd toast our cups of water and say grace over the McNuggets. It was very moving. But, you know, depressing. But depression is a valid human emotion. They say that reality is for people who can't face drugs, but I'd go further. I'd say reality is for people who can't *face* drugs.

OPRAH: That's the same thing.

FRANZEN: Oh, yeah. Anyway, it was a difficult schedule, and we finally broke up, and I spent three years eating gravel and banging my head on a radiator. I imagine it's the way Pynchon must have written *Gravity's Rainbow*. My wife used to say that a social worker would turn us in for self-abuse. But actually we only allowed self-abuse once a week, on Saturdays. As Balzac used to say, with every emission, "There goes another novel."

OPRAH: Meaning masturbation.

FRANZEN: Yes, but what is the meaning of masturbation?

OPRAH: How did you support yourself?

FRANZEN: I tracked earthquakes in the seismic department at Harvard. It was an easy job because that part of Massachusetts isn't very earthquake-prone, so there was no actual earthquake while I was there. If there was, I was supposed to call the campus police. But it never happened. It was a pretty easy job, actually.

OPRAH: Barbra Streisand once told me—

FRANZEN: But I was alone a lot. When you work alone so much of the time you forget how to talk to another human being.

OPRAH: I can see that. Quincy likes to—

FRANZEN: But you learn to deal with it, to fetishize your solitude. But it was difficult. I'd write two hundred pages and then I'd read it back and want to kill myself. I'd get drunk on shot glasses of vodka. Only I'd use water instead of vodka, because I was broke. Do you have any idea how many shot glasses of water it takes to get drunk?

OPRAH: Yes, Julia Roberts once told me she has the same problem. I mean, what shampoo do you use?

FRANZEN: Me?

OPRAH: No, it was a rhetorical question.

FRANZEN: Oh. I use Head & Shoulders, followed by an herbal rinse.

OPRAH: You spent a lot of time on this book.

FRANZEN: Nine years. Not counting the thirty-two years before that living it.

OPRAH: How many pages did you throw out?

FRANZEN: Lots.

OPRAH: Hundreds?

FRANZEN: Thousands.

OPRAH: And you worked in an isolation tank.

FRANZEN: Yes. Until you've tried typing in an isolation tank, you have no idea how difficult it is to read pages with blurred ink. But what I did was, I'd put the laptop in a plastic bag and then type through the plastic. I got electrocuted three times. But it really takes being electrocuted two or three times to re-create the full dysfunction of a family during recessionary times. I imagine it's how Mark Twain wrote *Huckleberry Finn*.

OPRAH: I can understand that. Toni Morrison once told me—

FRANZEN: You see, my job is to address the culture and bring news to the mainstream, without TV. I don't even have a TV.

OPRAH: I know, you already said that.

FRANZEN: Because it's true. I'm only gonna do Charlie Rose. And maybe *Who Wants to Be a Millionaire?* and *Temptation Island*.

OPRAH: Why do you have reservations about appearing on my show?

FRANZEN: TV has killed off too many of my favorite writers. My friend Carlos Bentini—he was killed off by TV. He'd just bought a fifty-two-inch Sony Wega Widescreen. It fell on him. He hadn't even gotten it working yet. It was tragic.

OPRAH: I see.

FRANZEN: I don't want a corporate logo on my book, either.

OPRAH: What about Farrar, Straus and Giroux?

FRANZEN: No, I had them take that off. I don't really like the term *book,* either. It's more than a *book*—it's really "a collection of words." Well, "words." I prefer "A collection of experiences, with a *New York Times* Bestseller Discount." Well, "Discount" . . .

OPRAH: What's wrong with an Oprah sticker?

FRANZEN: It brands you, and pretty soon you're in Wal-Mart and Costco, and men are coming up to you after readings and saying things like, "I saw your book at Wal-Mart" and "An awful lot of women seem to be reading your book." It's embarrassing. It's the way I imagine Bernard Malamud felt when Robert Redford turned up on his book jacket. I mean, that's not *Natural*. Ha ha. I just want to be free of everything that is branded or codified in any way.

OPRAH: I know what you mean. I have a Gulfstream IV. Do I need a V? No way. Not yet, anyway. Simplify, folks! Am I right?
(The crowd whoops and cheers.)

FRANZEN: I don't even have a car. I once walked the fourteen hundred miles from Eugene, Oregon, to Fairbanks, Alaska, to get the right tactile feeling so I could write the scene where Chip goes out for cigarettes in the 7-Eleven during the snowstorm.

OPRAH: I don't remember that scene.

FRANZEN: Because I cut it out. I spent fourteen years on this book, and twelve of them were spent strapped to the back of a tractor trailer, with my head and arms hanging down like mud flaps. It's the way I imagine Tolstoy wrote *Anna Karenina*.

OPRAH: Okay, well I'd like to open this up to my very patient audience here. Anyone have any questions for Jonathan? Yes, you in the back . . .

WOMAN IN THE BACK: Jonathan . . . Who do you see playing Chip in the movie? I think Jon Cusack would be great!
(Laughter in the audience.)

FRANZEN: That's it—I'm out of here!
(Franzen storms off.)

FAY WELDON

THE EVIL PAJAMAS: A Hampton Catalogue Murder Mystery

It was a cold night, dank and frosty, and Dorrie Blumskin was glad she was wearing her thermal long underwear, available in all sizes, in kooky peach and fun lime, at 32.00.

She heard a car drive up and peeked out the window to see her lover, Coates Bennett, pull up in his Jaguar XKJ. Quickly she peeled out of her long underwear and put on a satin and lace chemise, available in ivory, white, or whisper pink.

Coates opened the door. He was wearing a Royal Oxford Dress Shirt of luxurious texture with a brilliant finish. Handcrafted of premium two-ply Royal Oxford cotton and finished with a classic spread collar in your choice of French or button cuffs. Imported, in yellow, pink, gold, blue, lavender, and white, 35.00.

"Is that the new Cat Tin Roof slip?" he asked her.

"No, it's the Candy chemise, with double spaghetti straps. Also with a matching robe, from Intimates."

"Very sexy."

"And it doesn't fade or shrink with repeated washings."

They tore off each other's clothes and slipped into the bed, under the Fieldcrest washable down comforter, in twin, full/queen, or king.

Their passionate lovemaking was assisted by the Hampton Beginner's Bondage Set, with riding crop and handcuffs in stainless steel, so no rusting to hurt your tender wrists and ankles.

Afterwards, as they held each other in silence, Coates stared up at the ceiling.

"Penny for your thoughts," Dorrie whispered.

"I was just thinking how good the Hampton Catalogue customer service is," he said. "I once bought a Handwoven Silk Sportcoat, a perennial favorite, tailored of 100-percent silk in a subtle basket-weave pattern with center vent, two-button front, and three open patch pockets. Imported and fully lined, in Melon, 140.00."

"What was wrong with it?"

"Absolutely nothing. Except that I'd ordered it in a 42 Long, which was much too big. Anyway, they offered me a full refund or store credit. I returned it for a 38 Short. No problem at all. And look at these pajamas."

Dorrie looked at the pajamas, which Coates took with him wherever he went, carrying them in his leatherette briefcase, Salmon Pink and Veal Tan, 120.00 from Bag End.

"These PJs, made of the softest 100-percent cotton, never feel rough on my skin. Also, the waistband has reinforced elastic."

"So it doesn't lose its shape."

"Exactly. And what was it you said about your chemise?"

"No shrinking or fading."

"Bingo. So too with these pajamas, a Hampton exclusive, in white, blue, river, or khaki, with point collar and contrast piping inside. Incredible craftsmanship, at only 60.00 a pair."

"Dreamy," said Dorrie, running her fingers along his collar. Strange, she thought, it feels a *little* rough. Maybe he used the wrong detergent.

The next morning Dorrie awoke to a curious silence. Coates usually snored (forcing Dorrie to switch on her Ambient Noise Machine, 45.00, available from Superfluous Appliances), but this morning there was nothing but eerie silence. She looked over and saw he was unnaturally still. She kissed him on his left ear. It was stone cold.

Was Coates really dead? To make sure, Dorrie fetched her Kwik-Korpse-Tester (28.00, available in Sage, Storm Blue, Lavender, Orange, Black, and Maize) and attached the mask to Coates's face. Sure enough, the meter read "D."

Then she noticed, for the first time how faded Coates's pajamas looked—as if he'd left them in the sun for weeks. Not only that, they clung to him like a clenched, second skin—they'd actually shrunk in the middle of the night, the sleeves barely reached the wrists, the leg cuffs stopped short of his ankles by three inches at least, the buttons dug into his stomach like screws. Dorrie realized with a shock that *Coates had been suffocated by his own pajamas.*

But how was that possible? Hadn't he said himself that his sleepwear was a Hampton exclusive? Didn't he announce pride in the craftsmanship that had gone into making it?

She reached over to the collar to read the label. Maybe, as with the silk sportjacket, Coates had ordered the wrong size. Was he actually wearing a Small? A Medium?

Dorrie had trouble reading the label—the words were small and in tiny Aristocrat type. No, it was an "L." But what's this? *Harpton?* The pajamas were not from Hampton at all but a cheap knockoff joint!

Had Coates been fooled? Or had he deliberately bought a phony product? How could a man with a Jaguar wear cheap pajamas?

Dorrie would never know. But what would she do now? Coates's body was already turning blue.

Luckily, Dorrie had registered with the Hampton Stiff Remover® (HSR) Service, and the van was there in less than 30 minutes. Not bad, she thought, for only 12.00 per month.*

---

*Rates may vary depending on your location and state of corpse.

TOM WOLFE

PUFFY COMBS IS THE NEW DUKE OF SEANHAMPTON!

Pock . . . Pock . . .

On a crew-cut lawn so immaculate it looks like the green felt of a pool table, Sean Combs, a.k.a. Puff Daddy, a.k.a. Puffy, a.k.a. P. Diddy, the potty-mouthed, gun-toting, cap-busting Bad Boy brotha is . . . playing croquet.

Pock!

He's wearing a floor-length mink coat over a white velvet track suit, about fifteen pounds of gold jewelry, and white Nike Airs. It's mid-July. He's got a thirty-six-room "cottage" on twenty acres of landscaped grounds in Southampton. Do you realize how much twenty acres, on the right side of Route 9, in Southampton *costs?* Well, as they say, if you have to ask, you can't afford it.

Puffy can afford it. He is the hip-hop impresario of gangsta rap, the boombox soundtrack to the urban thug life, with a net worth in the millions.

He's playing with his homeys Donald Trump (D. Trump-Diddy?), Bobby de Niro (Bobby D-Ro?), and Barbara Walters (B. Wa-Wa?). The director of the Guggenheim is coming in this afternoon. Kissinger just left this morning.

"Don't be knockin' my ball, Bickle."

De Niro waves a hand and flashes his psychotic grin.

Pock!

Puffy is the Duke of the new Southampton. Call it Seanhampton. He is F. Scott Fitz-Daddy. Black is the new black.

As he plays croquet, holding the mallet "Puff-style" like a golf club, he recites his personal business haiku:

Time is money to me.
I want you to have the flavor.
Be cool.

Despite the small party, it's still not exactly an intimate afternoon in the Hamptons; Puffy's six Nubian bodyguards—half advance team, half security detail—shadow his every move. He's dressed them in Oxfords, striped jackets, white shirts, school ties (Harrow or Eton, judging by the stripes), and *boaters*. It looks as if a bunch of Green Bay Packers just swallowed the Princeton Glee Club. One hundred and twenty-fifth Street meets Merchant-Ivory. Harlem-cum-Henley Regatta. *Ghetto Fabulous.*

You gotta
grab the motherfucker by the small hairs.
Know what I'm sayin'?

Back in the days of the Flack-catchers and the Mao-Mao Gang, a thorny problem was how to throw a party for the Black Panthers without using black servants. But white help in 1966 was, as the English say, a little "thin on the ground." Hoards of Mexican immigrants had to be bused to the Upper West Side, fitted with white uniforms, and taught how to hold a tray.

This is no longer a problem. Father Combs calls his entire retinue his "posse," and it's a social construct with roots in the utopian agrarian communes of New England in the nineteenth century. No one takes as an insult the requests to hustle up some female companionship, because the ensuing bacchae will be to the good of the whole community. And although Pater Combs always has the corner office, as it were, he is more Big Brother than Boss Man of the Big House. It may be true that the man has Negritude—in spades. But there's another side of the Puff, that might be described as *Noblesse Baises-Toi*. And he has *arrived*.

Just don't piss him off. People who have pissed Puffy off have tended to get hurt. There was the video producer who filmed the Puff in an unflattering light (or so Mr. Combs claimed). He got a bottle smashed over his head. Puffy was acquitted.

But then, Puffy gets acquitted of everything. Nine people killed during a stampede at a Combs-sponsored celebrity basketball game? Acquitted! Arrested on bribery and illegal gun possession? Acquitted! He lives a solid-gold charmed life; he has a Get-Out-of-Jail-Free card. (Actually, it's pretty expensive.)

But what does Puffy want?

W
H
A
T

D
O
E
S

P
U
F
F
Y

W
A
N
T
?

WhAt DoEs PuFf Y wAnT?

Maybe all he wants is a little respect (or "spect," as they say in the ghetto). Puffy wants class, and if you don't have time to arrive on the *Mayflower,* why not buy a seat in the Hamptons? In *A Night at the Opera,* Mrs. Teasdale (Margaret Dumont) was attempting a similar maneuver with the help of Otis P. Driftwood, the conniving business adviser played by Groucho Marx. Driftwood recommended that Mrs. Teasdale underwrite the New York Metropolitan Opera to get into Society.

Seventy years later, opera is not *the shit,* and the admission to Society is made significantly easier by the cognoscenti angling to add a bit of "street cred" to their dull lives. Thus, Old Wealth and the wrinkly descendants of the Newport 400 vie for a photo op with the ganstas of the New Millennium.

In this capacity, Puffy Combs is the chicky-baby. He's accepted a position as Guest Lecturer of Musicology at Harvard. His recent (ghostwritten?) collection of *New Yorker* "casuals" has been published by Knopf. And he just released a CD of duets with the likes of Frank Sinatra, Dean Martin, and Sammy Davis Jr. ("Rat Pack from Beyond the Grave"), which may well hit the Top Ten—with or without a bullet. But his cap-busting, shoot-em-up days are over. The man is growing *orchids,* for godsake!

Consider the homeys who have played with him in his crib. The guest list of his last party (a fund-raiser for—whatever. Who cares?) could have been culled from the donors list of both the National Republican Committee and National Public Radio. *The Diddy's Gone National!* Last week, partaking of the shiitake mousse and Cristal champagne under Puffy's white tent, you could have run into Alan Dershowitz, Marlon Brando (in a gold muumuu), James Baker (still hair-challenged), Al D'Amato, Mayor Bloomberg, Arthur Miller, Barbra Streisand (smoking a cigar), Tom DeLay, Sting, Francis Coppola, F. Lee Bailey, Jerry Seinfeld, Stephen Sondheim (and friend), Margaret Thatcher (at least it looked like her), Charlie Rose (interrupting everyone), Jean-Luc Godard (or was it Cher?), Jerry Lewis (is he still alive?), Rupert Murdoch, Jim Carrey (pretending to be Dustin Hoffman), Dustin Hoffman, Peter Jennings (posing in avuncularity), Binky Urban, Jonathan Franzen (complaining that he shouldn't have been invited), Ted Kennedy,

Jeremy Irons, Gwyneth Paltrow (thin as a toothpick), Ed Burns, Christy Turlington, Sean Connery, Rush Limbaugh (speaking too loudly), William Weld (who?), Cate Blanchett (Queen of the Elves), Arianna Huffington, Newt Gingrich . . .

Does he have any, uh, black friends? "Yo, White Suit—some of my best *niggaz* are black!" Okay. But most of his best niggaz are white. "You got a problem wid dat?"

The Guggenheim director finally arrives in a black Town Car. "Sorry I'm late, P. Diddy. Traffic was terrible."

"Shoulda taken my chopper," says Puffy. "I would of had you picked up if I knew you'd be so late. Grab a mallet and join my crew."

After a few plays it's clear that Guggenheim is no croquet whiz.

"Yo, Googie, how about doing a Sean John show at your shell crib?"

"Sean John?"

"My clothing line. It's the shit, yo."

Guggenheim laughs.

"I'm serious. You did Armani."

"Well, that was Armani," says the director.

"And he kicked in some moolah, I know. I heard your museum's in real trouble."

"That's not strictly—"

"So say I nosed a little green your way. Gave you a Puffy Grant."

And the director is laughing again, doubled over, on his knees. He reaches out and touches Puffy on his leg. Immediately, one of the bodyguards grabs the curator's hand.

"Don't touch Mr. Combs."

The curator retracts his hand. "No, it's just that . . . well, Armani is considered an artist."

"Yo, and I guess I'm a grease monkey at Burger King."

"No . . ."

"And what about that Microsoft shit, sponsored by Bill Gates? What was that about?"

"That was a case of synergistic marketing."

"And Disney? I suppose Mike Eisner didn't fix no lightbulbs, yo."

"They were very helpful."

"Your move."

The curator looks sullenly down at his croquet ball. He gives it a tap with his mallet, sending it gliding through a hoop until— *clock!*—it smacks into Puffy's gold, monogrammed ("S.C.") ball. A shudder runs though the curator's shoulders.

One of the Glee Club bodyguards steps in front of the director. "Don't touch Mr. Combs's ball."

"It cool, it cool," says Puffy. "It all good, yo."

Placing a foot on his own ball, Puffy lifts his mallet high as if preparing for a golf tee-off—and smashes it below his foot.

Sssssssssssssssssoockkkkkkkkkkkkkkkkkkkk!!!

The curator's ball goes sailing across the lawn, across the path, and plops into the Olympic-sized, phallic-shaped swimming pool. The curator turns red.

"Hope you got goggles," says Puff. The posse laughs.

Friends say Combs was inconsolable after Jennifer Lopez (J.Lo) left him, but he seems pretty consolable now. Since February he's been seeing Mia Farrow, the delicate bird with the retractable claws. "She got a whole posse of kids," he says incredulously. (He's also been linked with Helena Bonham Carter, Kate Winslet, and Kristin Scott Thomas, but that was during his so-called U.K. phase.)

Although Father Combs has a couple of his own issue, he has mailed them securely off to a boarding school in England (Brigfield in Sussex) and doesn't expect to see them again till they get married, perhaps twenty years hence. Thus his "Daddy" moniker refers more to his current position as father figure to his adult retinue than to his actual offspring. Ms. Farrow evidently hasn't quite grasped this concept, having just adopted her seventeenth child—a thirteen-year-old blind Muslim girl who was rescued (*burqua* and all) from a refugee camp in Pakistan.

"It's not that I don't like *children*," Puff explains. "It's just that I don't like them around me. In concept, they good."

"You mean, in *conception,* they good," a plus-size flack remarks.

Puff holds out his flat palm, which Plus-Size slaps (a maneuver known in the parlance as "delivering a five").

Pock!

Is he trying to tell us something? Does he really just want to be left alone, after all? Is the pressure to always be *the shit* of the moment finally getting to him?

Everything all good.
I mean, we still cool.
It all good.

"Yo, Puff, it's Mia," says Plus-Size, holding out a gold-plate, wafer-thin Motorola cell phone.

"What she want?"

"She says she's going to be late. She gotta bring one of the kids to the vet."

"Which one?"

"The new Indian girl."

The Puff-man smiles. "She kind of cute, that one."

Pock!

The sun has fallen behind the pool house, so Puffy has the ground lights switched on, bathing the estate in the glow of a small airport. Puffy has turned night into day! None of the neighbors dares complain.

Face it—this brotha is the new Rockefeller, and he is bringing his ways to your mall (as well as, of course, to the Guggenheim: "Sean Jean: A Retrospective" coming to the museum next year). Crass? You don't get it, do you? This orchid-growing, party-giving, white-furball mogul is throwing his success right in your honky-ass face! *You got a problem wid dat?*

Pock!

RICK MOODY

LAUNDROMAT AMERICA

He who has put his clothes in a laundry bag, who has taken his soiled attire down to the Laundromat, who has balanced the bag on his shoulders, carried his besmirched carrion, the burden of life lived in the sweat of the week; he who has washed his clothes, dried them, and then folded them—*he shall verily be blessed and have clean clothes.*

He arrives prostrate under the burden of his heavy bag, tied by a slipknot, steps down the stone stairs, opens the door, and enters the steaming sanctuary of flickering fluorescence with its fetid, chemical air. He nods to the kind Korean owner flipping through the *Post,* this benevolent priest of this buzzing way station for tired citizens dirt-weary with ring-around-the-collar—strangers brought together by the soiling of their vestments, *brought together by their very humanness and need to smell clean.*

He carries the bag to the machine, opens the porthole, and puts in his offerings of a blemished week:

the Levis 501 jeans (OHM, lower Broadway, $34.95 on sale) with the pale blue of Cezanne's Mont Sainte-Victoire in the evening, faded and bepatched, w. 34, l. 32;

the black cords, their plated threads worn down and ruptured; his blue sweat pants with the double striped lines running down the legs, the ski tracks going nowhere;

his Ramones T-shirt, which he bought at a record store in the East Village[1] in 1984 for six dollars—the logo faded, the picture of the Ramones cracked and webbed like a Roman vase,[2] the image a Pentimento from another era—the shirt worn and washed and worn and washed again, cleaned like absolution;

his Swedish Kafka T-shirt ("Kafka hade imte heller sa rolight")[3]

his Black Dog T-shirt;[4]

his Lollapalooza T-shirt;[5]

his socks in twos, like Noah's chosen beings, some threadbare and toe-holed, some missing their mates, sock widows in mourning for their amputated love, small foot soldiers of shredded fabric—he drops one, no two, on the floor, and retrieves them and puts them in the machine,[6] with

his Calvin Klein boxers and boxer-briefs[7]

assorted linen, including the green Kmart towels and washcloths, the bath mat and kitchen towels, the black sheets and pillow cases.

---

1. Joey Ramone, that traveling troubadour of troubled youth, murmuring mumbler of Day-Glo punk obviousness, that garbled alphabet that spelled his domicile CBGB with his Bowery brethren burping bandinage, gangly guitarist too tall for his T-shirt, singing his song in Methodist orthodontia, like a pigeon exploding over Elizabeth, New Jersey.

2. See footnote 6.

3. "Kafka didn't have such a good time either."

4. A souvenir his ex-girlfriend Molly Stromburg bought him on a trip to Martha's Vineyard, which he prized and proudly wore until he realized that everyone else in the Village seemed to have the same shirt, the dog a black silhouette, a dog in negative form, the outline of a dog—*an undog*—the sleeves shriveled, now formless and unattractive.

5. $20 from the second tour, purchased after the Chili Peppers's sharp if rushed set, but stained with ketchup by a bystander's rambunctious and likely overpriced hot dog.

6. See footnote 2.

7. Calvin Clean, Calvinist Kind, Kal-Can, Can Can, can-do cleanliness, clean manliness, cleanliness is next to Godliness.

He who takes out his wallet and discovers he has no cash, goes to the ATM—a bank rendered in gray plastic, miniaturized to something smaller than a cigarette machine (a species now extinct, banned nationally, though he missed the tactile experience of it—two parts slot machine, one part pinball—the sharp pull of the plastic knob, the *za-zonk!* of the packet falling to the metal tray below) to which he slips in his bank card and taps out the modern Morse of instant fiduciary pleasure—delivered in the crisp bills of virgin commerce. But he needs coins and goes to the change machine *(This machine is for customers only)* that sucks dollar bills and spits out quarters in Las Vegas thrill—*ding-ding-ding-ding*—paper money broken into its base form, crushed into socialist change, chopped into quarters, the communion wafers of Laundromat America.

He inserts the coins, the weekly offering, thinking of the names of the detergents as hopeful saints (Tide, Fad, Cheer, Downy, Clorox, Bounce, Ivory Snow, Arm & Hammer), he who has brought the small glass jar of turquoise liquid, the smell of lavender gasoline, and pours this pungent syrup into the open metal hatch of the top drain—*he shall be doing sundry Laundromat things.*

He sits on one of the candy-colored plastic seats and peruses the tattered signs taped on the wall, urgent calls for lost dogs, Spanish lessons, Tai Chi classes, meditation centers, "Free Your Voice," VCR for sale, Room for Rent—*the messy call of capitalism, the drumbeat of democracy.* He thinks how clothes die once a week, but are reborn, baptized in sudsy waters, purified and fabric-softened.

The clothes are spun dry, and he fetches a metal ribbed cart and pushes it over to the washing machine, opens the porthole, and pulls out the wet clump, spilling them into the basket. He pushes the basket over to a dryer and tosses in the damp apparel, with a couple of sheets of Bounce, that magic chemical tissue that banishes static cling. For a short while, after inserting four quarters, he stands and watches the spinning drum, mesmerized by the industrial monotony, lulled by its warm hum. *Eventually, realizing his standing won't make his laundry dry any faster, he searches for something to read.*

His eyes fall on the pile of free weeklies, the timorous tabloids of urban squeal. He takes one from the tidy stack and peruses it: a compendium of film reviews and lonelyhearts advice. He wonders who reads the columns and what happens to the unread copies. Are they collected once a week, as the new issue is delivered, and pulped? Are they recycled? Are they dumped in trash cans from whence they are retrieved by homeless folk *and used for wall insulation in the mole world of the underground?*

The weekly paper cycle matches his own laundry routine, as if the newspapers are produced for his own personal amusement and edification. They are the Gideon Bibles of the Laundromats, updated weekly, adapted to the pulse of the times.

He feeds more quarters into the dryer until his duds are fried and steaming. Pulling out his underwear he can smell the burnt fabric—when he folds them, *the elastic in the waistbands snaps gently like crisp toast.*

He folds everything, slowly, methodically, a ritual of singular concentration. He appraises his touch of the clothes, the smell of the air, the look of the light dulled off the metal surfaces of the machines. He thinks about how he feels. He wonders if he intellectualizes everything too much, even intellectualizes emotion— *even intellectualizes his own intellectualizing.*

He carefully packs the neat piles of apparel and places them in his nylon laundry bag, slinging it over his shoulder. Verily he has delivered unto himself clean clothes, but he knows the task is not over. In a week he will be back, to be cleansed again, of the vestments destined to return. It is the cycle of life, the Sisyphean task of trying to stay hygienically sound.

CORMAC McCARTHY

ALL THE PRETTY SENTENCES

The wet of the rain fell like water falling hard on the wet rocks of the corral as they rode through the corral under the harsh hack of the clouds which looked o'er them menacingly. It was just the two of them riding as they had ridden hundreds of generations for thousands of years afore them.

Grizz said they mind as well stop in at a picture house as there weren't likely to be no holding aback of this rain. Clod nodded to Grizz and didnt say anything. They rode on alookin for a Rialto or a Bijou only there weren't none open just the old Plainville Drive-in. So they went in there sittin on the horses and affixin their radios to get them the sound of the picture.

The picture they watched involved this girl see who fell in love with the wrong guy. The right guy was her best friend which even a blind person could see but the girl couldn't see it. Here he was right under her nose only perhaps that was the problem as maybe he was too close for her to notice. So she goes and marries the no-good guy who cheats on her and becomes a drunk, losing all their money to the dog track. She's forced to take in washing and it's a tough life and she means to confront her husband to tell him that she's leavin him but he goes crazy and starts swiping at her with one of the fireplace tongs. He sure looks like he's gonna kill her only while tryin to swipe her he falls back on a metal shelf bracket in the wall and is killed instantly. She's in a big mess over that and is tried for his murder in a long courtroom scene that goes on for a while. Finally she's acquitted by a surprise witness who happened to see the proceedings through the window across the street. And there's amuch cheerin and a-hollerin in the courtroom and they would of flung their hats in the air if any of them of had hats. And she turns around and there sittin quietly in the back is her old best friend who she now realizes she'd taken for granted. And she goes over to him and they hug and go out for brunch and then some and pretty soon they are fixin to get married. Only now he got only six months to live on account of the cancer. And they get married anyway and have a good time of it though it's a short time and the good guy starts coughing and dies in her arms and she's bawling like a baby. And you can tell that she really loved him all along.

Clod and Grizz were cryin too and both the horses were cryin but it was lucky for the rain as nobody could see the tears as they roll off their faces.

That was a good picture, said Clod.

That film was okay, said Grizz as he smoked a cheroot. Only I didn't believe the bit about the metal shelf bracket. Seems to me you might be bruised slightly if you fell back on a metal shelf bracket but I don't think you'd be killed by it.

The thing that probably happened, said Clod, is that it was the shock that killed him.

What shock?

The shock of being knocked off his balance. And then hitting the shelf bracket. It's a surprise for a man to be knocked like that.

He wasn't knocked, said Grizz. He just fell back. It was hard to believe in that part of it and it ruined the picture for me.

It lacked all verisimilitude, said Clod.

Verisiwhat?

Militude.

Oh yeah, said Grizz. It lacked that.

They were saying this as they rode out of the drive-in and back into the corral. Grizz had finished the cheroot and tossed what was left of it on the ground. It was even darker now and the wet rain had stopped falling on them as a soft haze rose up from the ground gently bathing them in an essence of viscosity. Clod and Grizz stopped talking as it could have ruined the calmness of the quietude of the corral. Clod thought about the horses and wondered if they had the same problem with the picture as he did. He thought a movie without a horse must be a boring thing to a horse because a horse is a horse of course of course.

Clod's horse was a brown one with very short fur and a long tail that whipped and swished this way and that way when they went walkin as they did quite frequently at that particular juncture. Grizz's horse was a black one with similar short fur.

Clod rode right behind Grizz when they had to go single file on the narrow bike path. He watched as Grizz's horse's tail lifted and a powerful pack of equestrian essence came forth and unto the earth plopping from the firmament and furthering the majestic cycle of life. The horse's nostrils flared in pride as he knew he was bestowing a great gift on the plain where it was painful to grow and difficult to cultivate and yet here was the very gift of life itself even on a bike path.

They were lookin to go gold prospectin at the old silver mine outside Ghostville by the Mexican border with Mexico. Word gone out through the territory that a man could make hisself some serious dinero the old-fashion way if he was willing to put in the work. The jovenes today didn't know how to work and they didn't know how to play neither. The jovenes were too estúpido to know what it was to live a life that had to be lived. Clod figured he'd work on the silver mine and get hisself enough gold to retire at thirty-five or maybe forty-five depending on which came first. Then he could go back to his first love which was carnival barking. He'd barked carnivals from Besmirch Texas to Donkeyglue Arizona and everyone said he was the best damn carny barker since Mad Dog Jesus the Spanish barker from Cajones Mexico.

He was thinkin this when a one-eyed woman stopped them on the plain where they were now having come off the bike path. She

was a good-looking woman with the exception of the one eye and
with her was a young woman likely her daughter who had the
usual number of two eyes. Clod quickly calculated that between
them the women had three eyes.

Where you headed? asked the one-eyed woman.

Ghostville, said Clod.

No good. Aint nothing there. S'all gone.

We're gold prospectors, said Clod.

The one-eyed woman laughed a crazy laugh and slapped her
right thigh in a right thigh-slapping gesture.

The two men figured she was a crazy woman and so on account
of this they took the other woman who was probably a puta.

You come with us, said Clod.

He tied the young, two-eyed woman to his saddle. She said
nothing but hummed slightly to herself a tune that Grizz thought
might be "Is That All There Is?" or perhaps "Tax Man."

What you gonna do with the puta?

Gonna sell her at Ghostville. Maybe get a couple of shovels for
her.

They rode on not saying anything for a while. The puta was sleeping peacefully across Clod's saddle. Before them was the terrible
sharp flatness of the plain as the sun burned red and low on the
horizon and the shimmering air turned still and calm and humble.
They stopped on a road and watched as the majestic vultures or
maybe they were pigeons glided in circles until they swooped down
and picked up the jackrabbits or possibly ferrets it was hard to tell
in the dust. It was an awesome sight whatever it was even if it was
nothing.

I werent gonna bring this up, said Grizz. But I don't rightly see
as the puta is yours to sell.

She's just a puta. What does it matter?

A puta is still a person whether she's a puta or not.

Maybe.

You know I'm right on this and I try not to bug you about stuff
that aint inessential and I'd say more only I'm running out of
prepositions.

Clod thought of the vultures or maybe pigeons and he thought what a hard world it was especially if you were a puta. And he thought about Grizz's problems with a lack of prepositions and he wondered what he meant by that.

Near the Mexican border with Mexico they realized they were lost. They flagged down a Mexican who was riding on a caballo. He stopped and Clod and Grizz got off their horses and the Mexican got off his caballo and Grizz told the Mexican about the puta who was still asleep on Clod's saddle. The Mexican was interested but not too interested as it wasn't exactly his line of work. The Mexican said he was a cowpuncher and that the cows loved being punched. He said you haven't punched a thing until you punched a cow and after the cow was punched he thanked you in the only way a cow can thank you and it usually involved phlegm. He said that when a cow phlegms you after it's been punched it's a lovely thing that no one can take away from you no matter how long you live or where you go. He said that after he punched a cow and got phlegmed by it they often sat down together to play cards or watch a movie. Or at least Clod thought that's what he said because the Mexican was speaking in Mexican and Clod's Mexican werent so good.

Clod handed over the puta to the Mexican and the Mexican thanked the men and got back on his caballo and rode away. For many hours afterwards the men made fun of the Mexican cow-puncher's accent going *Arriba arriba* and *Ándale ándale*.

The men were still lost and there was no sign to Ghostville. It was raining again and there weren't no drive-ins or even covered picture houses to take shelter in so they looked for a motor lodge to spend the night. At a Motel 6 they brought the horses inside and had them sleep on the fold-out couches that dipped in the middle where so many people had slept in them for so many years. The brown horse kept getting up in the middle of the night to go to the bathroom and also leaving the light on in the bathroom so the men couldn't get to sleep.

You up? asked Clod.

Am now, said Grizz. He lit a cheroot and began smoking the cheroot.

I'm telling you Grizz you're lookin at one weary cowboy.

I'm not lookin at you, said Grizz. He was still smoking the che-root and he tapped out some ash on the carpet.

I'm tired of a life without commas, said Clod.

Sometimes we get a comma when we speak, said Grizz.

Aint enough, said Clod. A man needs a comma more than just when he's speaking. Aint nothing queer about a comma. It's just a matter of what you do with it. But a life with a lot of run-on sen-tences and no commas—it just aint natural.

Clod whistled. Wow, that were quite a dash you got there.

Why, thank you, Clod.

And Grizz knew he was right—that punctuation was just as manly as no punctuation at all, and that grammar could be a guy's best friend, besides a horse. Maybe they'd get to Ghostville and maybe they'd go to the grammar rodeo over in Harlan; their options were truly limitless.

Henceforth they would shorten their sentences, and add com-mas, and just thinking this made them contented. As it did the horses, who finally went to sleep, snoring occasionally as horses are wont to do. Grizz thought the sound was like a lullaby, and he finally went to sleep too. (Clod was already asleep.)

NICHOLSON BAKER

BOX

"What are you doing?" he asked.

She said, "I'm sitting in a box."

"What kind of box?"

"Just a box. I got it with the twenty-seven-inch Sony Trinatron TV I bought at—"

"Stay with the box," he said.

"Oh, okay. You want me to describe the box?"

"Yes."

"It's, um, *cardboard* . . ."

"What kind of cardboard?"

"What kind?"

"Is it corrugated?"

"Yes."

"Is it rough on your skin?"

"Sort of."

"Are you naked?"

"Yes. Naked in the box."

"Are you wearing socks?"

"Yes. My socks are in the box."

"Good."

"Should I be eating lox? Should I be in detox? Suffering from the pox?"

"Don't try to be amusing."

"Am I sly as a fox? Is this a series of shocks?"

"Come on . . ."

"I've lost all my stocks. Are you getting off your rocks?"

"I'll hang up if you keep on like this."

"Sorry, sorry . . . But when opportunity knocks . . ."

"That's it." He was about to hang up.

"Wait!"

"Are you ready to be serious?"

"Yes. I'm in the box. Sitting in my socks." She giggled, but recovered. "The interior is smooth."

"Oh. What color is it?"

"The box? It's, uh, *brown.*"

"What kind of brown."

"Uh . . . chocolate brown?"

"Okay. Milk or dark?"

"Milk?"

"*Milk* chocolate or *dark* chocolate?" He was getting impatient.

"Oh. I guess *milk* chocolate."

"It's smooth on your skin?"

"Yes."

"Can people see you?"

"Not really. The box is on the floor."

"Is your ass cold?"

"No. My ass is sticking to the bottom of the box."

"Is your *pussy* stuck to it?"

"Not really. But my ass—"

"I think your pussy *is* stuck to it."

"Yes, you're right. It's completely stuck to the bottom of the box. I'm what you might call 'cunt-stuck.' "

"Stop it."

"But it's true. My cunt is stuck. I might have to call the fire department."

"Are your arms inside the box?"

"They are now."

BOX   197

"Play with yourself in the box."

"There's not much room . . ."

"*Play* with yourself."

"I am. I'm playing. Play play play."

"What are you doing?"

"I'm playing with myself. In the box."

"Describe it."

"I'm, uh . . . Pinching my nipples and rubbing up against the side of the box."

"Are there flaps?"

"Flaps?"

"On the box."

"Oh. Yes."

"Are they inside or outside the box?"

"Outside."

"Okay. I want you to scrunch down in the box and fold the flaps closed."

"Okay."

"Are you doing that?"

"Hold on . . ."

"Are you scrunched down in the box?"

"Yes."

"It's dark in there, isn't it?"

"It's pretty dark."

"What are you doing?"

"I'm trying to breathe."

"Are you being mailed?"

"Maled?"

"Mailed. Posted."

"Oh. No, I'm being sent UPS. My tracking number is 4973540 . . ."

"Are you on the truck?"

"I'm on the truck. *Vroom vroom.*"

"You're being knocked about in the back of the truck. There are other boxes."

"Oh yeah, it's box city here. We're having a box orgy. We're *boxing* . . ."

"That's good."

"It is?"

"Yes."

"Oh, we're boxing, all right. I'm getting KO'd by a split decision in the third round."

"Well, that's—"

"It's a TKO by a 7–3 in the second half . . ."

"Try not to get technical."

"I'm feeling *boxy*. My box has *moxie*."

"Hmm, I like this . . ."

"My box is getting *foxy*. I'm feeling *sexy* in my *soxy* . . ."

"Hmm, yes . . ."

"I'm getting soggy by proxy . . ."

"*Yes* . . ."

"The door's opening."

"What?"

"It's the UPS guy. He's wearing a pair of these little brown
shorts. He has very thick, muscular thighs . . ."

"Forget the UPS guy."

"But he's coming for me. He's picking me up. He's taking me
somewhere."

"He's taking you to a warehouse."

"No, it's a school."

"A school?" he said skeptically. "No, I think it's probably a
warehouse."

"I think I know the difference between a warehouse and a
school," she said indignantly.

"But you're inside the box. How can you see?"

"I'm peeking out of a hole in the side."

"You never mentioned a hole."

"Well I'm mentioning it now. I'm looking through the hole and
he's definitely taking me to a school."

"Okay, a school. Whatever. The UPS guy is carrying you into a
school."

"Yes. I can hear the chattering of children behind walls. I think
they're in a gym. They're playing that violent game where they
throw a ball at you."

BOX   199

"Basketball."

"Not basketball. They throw the ball directly at you, trying to hit you, then you're out."

"Oh. Dodgeball."

"Right, dodgeball. I remember having to play it at high school. I tried to hide, but the instructor, Miss Pinchley, yelled at me and made me come out to the open and I got hit so hard I had a purple welt the shape of Brazil for three weeks."

"Are you sure it was Brazil?"

"I think so. Why?"

"No, it's just that Brazil isn't really a very distinctive shape."

"It was on my welt. I should know what it looked like."

"Well, presumably you were looking at it upside down, unless the welt looked like Brazil upside down to other people. Or did it look like Brazil in the mirror, in which case it'd be Brazil in reverse?"

"Look, it was just a welt."

"Did you secretly enjoy getting it? Like a purple badge of honor? Are you into spanking?"

"I'm not into getting hit by a heavy rubber ball in my right thigh."

"What's that sound?" He could hear squeaking in the background.

"I'm being moved again. They must have brought me to the wrong address."

"What's the squeaking?"

"The handtruck squeaks."

He heard some banging and then a muffled grinding sound. "What's happening?"

"I'm back in the truck. We're moving."

"I once ordered something from one of the Adam & Eve catalogs."

"What was it?"

"Actually, it was a doll. One of those full-size sex dolls."

She was laughing. "You're not serious."

"It was a joke, really. But I was very curious. It's not so much that I expected to get off on it, exactly, but I was very interested to see how it might work."

"And did it?"

"Yes, but not in a sexual way. She turned out to be—"

"She?"

"Yes, Veronica. She turned out to be shorter than I'd expected, so she fit into a lot of the clothes my ex-girlfriend left behind. It was surprising how well she looked in them, actually, especially a little Nicole Miller black dress that showed off her terrific legs. The sex was acceptable—nothing more—but we liked to have dinner together and then watch TV, mostly old *Thin Man* movies and RKO musicals. I have a lot of tapes. She liked William Powell. She used to sigh every time she saw him. Well, it sounded like a sigh, but it was usually her air leaking out, so I'd have to inflate her a bit."

"Give her a blow job."

"Well, essentially."

"Do you still have her?"

"No, I . . . We were celebrating our first anniversary with a lovely candlelit dinner I'd prepared of tortellini with artichoke pesto and a superb Chilean wine, and . . ."

"What? What happened?"

"We were lifting our glasses in a toast and she must have gotten too close to the candle and she just . . . caught on fire. I put it out as fast as I could, but it was too late and . . . I had a little ceremony and buried her in a Dumpster behind the Wal-Mart."

"Why there?"

"Oh, I'd just gone there to see if they carried anything like that."

"Wal-Mart?"

"They claim to carry everything, from toe socks to automatic weapons. But they have some gaps."

"Evidently."

"So I ordered one from a new catalog. I wanted something more realistic."

"But it hasn't come yet."

He was laughing.

"What's so funny?"

"No, it's just that . . . Veronica had a difficult time coming. I'd lick her in this very demonstrative, counterclockwise manner."

BOX 201

"You gave the doll oral sex?"

"Veronica, yes. I wouldn't have minded it so much, but she always tasted like polyurethane."

"Did you sleep with her?"

"Oh no. She always stayed in the box. I used to talk to her in the box. Except for dinner and TV time and then occasional sex, she was always in the box."

"So this is a very specific fantasy for you."

"Not a fantasy, a . . . a remembering."

"When did you order the new one?"

"A few weeks ago."

"What did you order?"

"Something much more expensive, more realistic. You know, with voice recognition and speech capabilities."

"It's amazing what they can do nowadays."

"Oh yeah." He heard some bumping. "What's happening?"

"The truck has stopped . . . they're opening up the back door."

"How do your nipples feel?"

"Bumpy. I'm being carried. They're putting me on a handtruck again. I'm being wheeled into a building."

"A warehouse?"

"I don't think so."

"After Veronica caught fire I didn't think I could go through with another model that posed a fire hazard. So I ordered something more substantial."

"I think you made the right decision."

"I know, it's time to trade up. Veronica was fine for as long as it lasted. But I think it was just a plastic phase I was going through."

"I know what you mean. I used to be into *Star Wars* figurines, but now . . ."

"You're into the real thing."

She laughed. "Exactly. I have Darth Vader back in my living room. . . ." There was a pause.

"Hello?"

"I think I better hang up now. We've reached the apartment."

"Okay, nice talking to you."

"Same here."

"Soon."

"Yeah, soon."

As he hung up he heard the buzzer, and he walked, with great anticipation, to the door.

E. ANNIE PROULX

VOCABULARY CRIMES

Pusome Callifaster worked the lobster shift at Radio Reflex, shoveling music cartridges into the brooding furnace. He had the head of a cauliflower, with lips the lithe parchment of a sponge cake, his eyebrows the taut sails of flags unfurled. He stood seven feet, two inches in his stocking feet, with skin the texture of a Lockheed jet.

"This is Raa-dio Re-flex, ding-dong-dang . . ."

He hated his job, but he was too tall and fat to do anything else. The radiator muttered mucously in the corner, the window spattled and sporched in the humdrum gizzled evening. Callifaster flossed his canspeach abreast his namesake sock. It was not that he knew not what willed wood. Wondrous, trunk-filled, filleted in action dreaming, like a moat of leaves on a river seeded sallow, he read the daily newspaper tip-tapping topful treason. Through the columns of regimental type, his sandy soulful eyes went gleaming, through the advertisements of cake boxes and bashful stabs at beach balls and billiard booths. He thought of the way his mother fed him, buried in the blue velvet dirt of the frog mount of lackluster Lake Cristo, kissed of monumental malfeasance. Tall and lanky, Mrs. Callifaster was a card shark widow, raising three sons on a taxi dancer's salary. Late at night she'd lullaby the infant Pusome, partridge plump, to the radio, rocking him as "Molly McGee" came on KNR-Chicago. Many nights petty Pue dreamt of ancient fortresses, strong as the muscle tendons of sea goats boiled in ancient cauldrons. He would see himself the image of the ageless one as, athwart and abrazened, the tally-caster coast of crimson breeze bespoke its truthsome squeal.

"What knocks nearby?" he'd say to sanded, scented air.

"Quid pro quotient," would say the voice of timeless tranquility.

"Huh?"

Awakened out of the reverential reverie redolent of the putrid past, Pusome beshook himself in the cold casement of the somnolent studio. He smelled of a cough drop dropped on the impatient tongue of a baton-twirling majorette in Chipmunk, Montana. He liked to spin records from his yeast-infected youth ("Little Nanny No-Legs," "The Cartwheel Cancer Song"), and often brought vinyl singles to the station, to broadcast audio snapshots from his Pusome past. Unfortunately there were no turntables in the studio, only machines for plastic cartridges and computers that controlled every dot and dash (or more accurately, every zero and one) of the station's lackluster effluence.

Pusome had ordered a turntable from a dog-eared Radio Shack catalogue, his constant companion. It was his Gideon's Bible, his *Encyclopaedia Britannica*, his *Chicago Manual of Style* all rolled into one.

There was a knock on the door. Pusome arose, carrying his hefty bulk with the gracelessness of a drunk heron stumbling on a piece of pockmarked ice in Migraine, Alaska. He expected it was the turntable, dispatched by overnight Federal Express delivery. He opened the door.

"Mr. Cauliflower?"

"Callifaster."

The man, who Pusome couldn't help noticing was not in a FedEx uniform but wearing a nondescript gray suit, consulted a clipboard. "Callifaster, that's right. You're under arrest."

"Arrest?" said Pusome, his brow furrowed felicitously. "What for, my fine fearsome fellow?"

"Vocabulary crimes, with an especially egregious use of adjectives. Everything you say can and will be used against you. You have the right to consult your line editor."

"I don't have a line editor."

"Oh, right. Obviously. What kind of name is Pusome Callifaster anyway?"

"I made it up. It's onomatopoeic."

"That's enough of that. Your alliteration has been deemed excessive too."

Sultry sad, Pusome panged palpably as he followed the fulsome Fed out the door. "Dang," he declared.

DAVE EGGERS

A BACKBREAKING WORK OF
INCREDIBLE THINNESS

Preface to the 3rd Paperback Edition

1. The author has received a number of complaints—well, let's call them exuberant observations with a smidgen of consternation—regarding the eighteen different covers of the first and second paperback editions of this book. a) Let the author make it perfectly clear (in a non-Nixonian way) that he had nothing to do with this marketing ploy, and b) he never said "Collect the set!" as misquoted by the despicably inaccurate *New York Times* reporter Ed Shuyler, who has been duly sued and ridiculed on the McSweeney's Web site. (You can reach him at the *New York Times,* ext. 3970, or E-mail him at Ed.Shuyler@newyorktimes.com.) If you do "collect the set" (and why *would* you?), note that they may indeed become collector's items (each cover has a print run of only 200,000) and that almost all profits go to the author's unprofitable publishing company. The author is still living in a shipping crate in Carroll Gardens, Brooklyn, and has no plans to move into the loft duplex he bought on Crosby Street in SoHo (it's being sublet to one of the Baldwin Bros.—Biff or Happy, D.E. forgets which).

2. Many of you have written in inquiring after the brother, Toph—the "MacGuffin," so to speak, of this whole enterprise. Many girls (some actually women "of a certain age," as the expression has it) have asked to date him. Toph is well, we presume, having entered the Witness Protection Program to escape what he claims is excessive exploitation. Don't you believe it. D.E. is suing him for defamation of character.

3. Regarding various complaints about the style of the book—i.e., its slapdashness and general aren't-I-cute, self-deprecating/self-loving preciousness—the author feels your pain. The book was written in a furious six-week period, on a Froot Loops bender, and if the author had to do it all over again, he'd do it differently, including this new preface.

4. During the recent McSweeney's Rolling Thunder Review Tour, somewhere between St. Louis and St. Paul (or perhaps some other saint), the author, entirely against his better judgment and slightly the worse for wear having imbibed several glasses of fruit punch at a book signing, may have gone home with someone named Heather or Heller or Heathcliffe, and this said alleged "fan," after a night of disappointing sex, which won't be gone through here, stole an item of great personal value, namely a Scooby-Doo watch given the author by a prominent MTV personality (who shall go nameless here) to commemorate the author's cohosting of *Total Request Live* (a superb show that featured the Goo Goo Dolls, Ani de Franco, and, perhaps for the first time ever on MTV, Brian Eno's "Music for Airports." A tape of this show is available for $19.95 [VHS] or $24.95 [DVD]) from the McSweeney's Web site. Will the deranged worse-than-Mark-David-Chapman fan kindly RETURN the pilfered effects.

5. In consideration of the author as an unlikely sex object, it should be noted that this is not a calculated affectation to appear more desirable, and that Eggers has a normal sex drive, but really just wants to "settle down" with a nice girl from whatever side of the tracks.

6. And yet, groupie nookie is accepted in certain circumstances. (Read book for more clues.)

7. Sometimes I lie awake at night and look at a tiny spot on the ceiling over my bed, and I imagine that it's the planet Earth, and

I'm on another planet—or, more likely, floating in the tepid viscous
of free space—and looking down on our planet, on the East Coast
of the United States (originally a singular, now a plural), my gaze
telescoping into New York, specifically Brooklyn, my neighborhood and the top of my building peeled off, the ceiling of my bedroom rolled back, and I see myself staring up at . . . myself? And I
think: Is that all there is? *And what is it, anyway?* Okay, not a specific
point for this new prologue, but I think an interesting observation
all the same.

   8. It should be noted that yes, I realize that I've slipped to the
first person. (It's all part of my plot, hee hee!) Also, that I fully recognize the ridiculous pretentiousness of this opening prologue
gambit. But I should like to state categorically that I am not the
type of person who would write a prologue. (So rest easy.)

   9. This is an absolutely stunning, brilliant book! (Only kidding.)

   10. Gentle reader, go out and buy yourself a drink. Get smashed!
You deserve it. You are truly kissed by angels.

DAVID MAMET

HOW IT IS TO WRITE

When it has come to that time that one has sat down and said to oneself: Now it is the time to write, one may say, to oneself, this one needs to say, or to do: Yes. As the great statesman Winston Churchill (who, it must be said, won his battles not on the playing fields of Eton but in the battlefields of the Ardennes, and who, it is of interest to note, won his Nobel Prize, not for Peace, but for Literature) said, Always write as simply as possible. This is not a good policy—it is the only policy. When it has come to that time that one must need to say to oneself: Now. Yes. Okay. One must do it.

Thus, after I had directed a film, I wrote the book *How to Direct a Film,* as well as my many essay collections, children's books, poems, cookbooks, how-to's, travel guides, film scripts, and, of course, my plays. Indeed, it is my plays for which, I suppose, I am, at last, most famous, that have instilled in me my sense of dramatic structure, and allowed me to bring to my nonfiction a sense of that same urgency! and drama!

How to Write Prose

Even as I am teaching my students at Harvard (who have paid upward of $150,000 to learn—or more accurately, their parents have), they say, "Mr. Mamet. How is it that one may write as simply and directly as one such as you?" And I say to that, one must eschew obfuscation, ha ha. Be as clear and as grammatical as it is possible to do so. But do not, as one is wont to do, shrink from an overabundance of punctuation, such as commas, and the like. They are, as always, your punctuous "friends." One can then write many essays—or even books of essays—as quickly as yours truly, in a matter of minutes, especially if your name is David Mamet, as mine, indeed, is.

How to Write Dialogue in Plays and Films

The first thing it is of import to note is: Make sure that your dialogue is natural sounding. Does it sound "real?" And then: "What is real?" And then, also: "What is the meaning of life?" (No—just kidding.)

Firstly, do not, under any circumstances, use contractions in speech. "Why not?" you may ask (and rightly so). To which I respond: "Shut the fuck up." Thus the line:

"I can't stand it. Don't do it. I'm stumped." should be written thusly:

"I cannot stand it. Do not do it. Lo, I am stumped." I ask you, which is more natural sounding and goes more gently on thine ear? Did Shakespeare use contractions? Did Molière? I think not. The Stoics would agree with me on this.

Also, do not let your characters overlap their dialogue. Why not? Because it destroys the "rhythm" of the speech. Thus, the following exchange:

BOBBY: She's a bitch, Donny, a fucking—
DONNY *(overlapping)*: No, that's not true, Bobby, she's a fuckin' princess . . .

BOBBY *(overlapping)*: Go fuck yourself, Bobby, and fuck your car too.

Improved, it becomes:

BOBBY: She is . . .
DONNY: No . . .
BOBBY: Donny . . .
DONNY: Look . . .
BOBBY: Don . . .
DONNY: I . . .
BOBBY: But . . .
DONNY: Bobby . . .
BOBBY: Go fuck yourself, Donny, and fuck your car too.

It seems to take longer, but it actually "gets" you to the "essence" of the "meaning" of the speech "faster."

Actors and How to Treat Them

All actors are idiots. Treat them like shit and ye shall be respected. What is important is the *text*. Tell the actor to move in the proper places (i.e., "block" the scene) and tell them to speak the words *clearly*. All actors should be *good-looking* and not less than 5'8" (men) or 5'4" (women). (For more information on this, see my *Manual for Actors: Shut the Fuck Up*.)

Magazine Editors and How to Treat Them

All editors are idiots. Tell them not to change a *word* or *comma* of your text. *Who* is the author? *You*. Who is the idiot? *Them*.

How to Write Poetry

The thing about poetry is that it has shorter lines than prose. Thus, the above sentence, in poetry, reads as follows:

> *The thing*
> *about poetry*
> *is that it has shorter lines*
> *than prose.*

Or you can write a haiku, which looks something like this:

> *Write anything,*
> *there will be someone to read it.*
> *People are fools.*

EVE ENSLER AND ANNE RICE

THE VAMPIRE MONOLOGUES

I know you're scared. You're worried. It's understandable. I was worried too. I was worried about vampires. There's so much darkness and secrecy surrounding them, but what are they really like?

You cannot love a vampire unless you love teeth. You have to love the night. You have to be comfortable with formalwear and a body that's sometimes scrawny and over four hundred years old.

If your vampire were a vagina, what would it say?

"Are these teeth really necessary?"
"Why do I have to sleep fourteen hours a day?"
"Read my lips."
"More blood, please. Keep it coming."
"Why are you scared of me?"
"It only hurts the first time."
"Suck on this."

Nicknames for Vampires

"Vam"
"Drac"

"Count"
"Puncture"
"Blood Monkey"
"Goth"
"Bram"
"Kabuki Face"
"Vlad"
"Bela"

Favorite Songs of Vampires

"Like a Virgin"
"I Get a Bite Out of You"
"Let It Bleed"
"All You Need Is Blood"
"Lipstick Traces"
"Don't Go Staking My Heart"
"When I'm Nine Hundred and Sixty-Four"

The Woman Who Likes to Make Vampires Happy

I love vampires. Vampires pay me to dominate them, to excite them, to bring them virgins so they can drink their blood. I didn't begin this way. I began as a real estate broker. But I woke up one morning and found two little dots on my neck, and I discovered my inner vamp. Now I'm a veritable umpire of vampires. I settle domestic disputes and answer FAQs: Who gets to suck the baby-sitter tonight? How can I get the best dental coverage? Which blood banks give the best interest? How attentive are the maids at the Transylvania Hilton, and how much should I tip?

Vampire Facts

In the nineteenth century, girls who went with vampires were often ostracized by the rest of the community. Their new empowerment was feared by others and they were chased by angry mobs carrying torches of fire.

Vampire Mutilation

In many countries, violence against vampires is an almost daily occurrence. Vampires are often mutilated and killed by having a wooden stake driven into their hearts while they are sleeping. In parts of Romania, the ritual murder of vampires is a cultural phenomenon going back hundreds of years, creating a "generational cycle of violence."

How You Can Help

We'd like to end all violence against vampires around the world within four years. You can help.

You can organize a "V" Day in your town. Invite local celebrity vampires (Vampira, Gary Oldman, Christopher Lee, Rosie O'Donnell) and raise vampire consciousness. Give blood. Don't forget the undead. Save an afterlife today!

DAVID FOSTER WALLACE

INFINITE PEST

Year of the Iowa Writers' Workshop

November 4

Charlie M. Brownian Motion is still autocommitted to the crack halfway house, but asks for a tour anyway, which is enthusiastically conducted by Mrs. Benigna Polyp,[1] dressed in a mauve *Star Trek* uniform with cargo pockets large enough to hold ammunition for her Kalashnikov. "We are really a house *in utero,* dedicated to the crack connoisseur," says Mrs. Polyp. "We were featured last month in *Crack Aficionado* magazine." Brownian Motion likes the curtains, a jaunty ensemble of synthetic rayon and polyester[2] in Messerschmitt silver and black. Mrs. Polyp notices his obvious admiration and glows. "I see you've noticed

---

1. Not to be confused with Benjamin Plop, whose popular nautical shindigs often brought the fish police.
2. No actual need for a footnote here.

the drapes. Yes, I bought those at a police auction down at the N.W.A.R.O.T.C.I.R.T.[3] You wouldn't believe what I found sewn into the hem . . ." And she takes out of her pocket a small white envelope containing two capsules, salmon pink. "I'm saving these for a rainy day."[4]

Kerr Wott Blott looks into the eyes of Dingo Mango Dango and senses in there somewhere is the soul of an oncologist. "The thing is," he says, thinking of thingness, "I'm not sure you are catching my particular drift."

"And what particular drift is that?" says Dango.

"And what particular *fucking* drift is that?"

"Right."

"I found this book, and . . ." He trails off, trying to connect his TCP[5] cable to his R101 disaster. "Um . . . Could you hold this for a second?" He hands the zeppelin to Dango, who locates a certain schadenfreude weltschmerz on the wall hanging of the X-K>D>P_Pffeflel.[6]

"You see, there's this book . . ."

"Yes?"

"Called *Infinite Pest*." He thinks back to when he first found the book, in the third month of the Year of the Graduate Writing Program. It was a huge tome[7] with clouds on the cover, and he dropped the book on his foot, breaking three of his toes. That had led to a number of podiatrical problems, including tennis foot and golf toe. "I started reading it, and . . ."

"And what?"

"I couldn't seem to . . ."

"Seem to what?"

---

3. Niggaz with Attitude ROTC Independent Rapid Transit.

4. *Untitled*. Unfinished. UNRELEASED.

5. Totally Capable Police. Well, maybe not.

6. Sometimes pronounced "piffle."

7. Sorry, I thought I had something to add. Never mind.

"Seem to *fucking* what?"
"Yes."
"I don't know. Maybe I just don't get tennis."

Blott suddenly feels a need to get back to the book as soon as possible, to immerse himself in it, to slip into it as someone slips into a warm bath. Maybe it will make sense this time. Maybe he can finish it. "I have to go now," he says, limping onto a streetcar named Entropy.[8] The vehicle has just passed Lot 49 when he finds himself unaccountably crying. He opens his North Face nylon-padded book bag and unsheathes his copy of *Infinite Pest,* carefully sliding it onto the seat next to him.[9] The cover gives him a little woody. He opens to where he left off, the *Atlantic Monthly*. Lonely Hearts Reading Club bookmark tucked into page 3,969 . . . or is it 2,868? Or is it 4,262? He can't be sure—the pages seem to blur. Some are actually stuck together.[10] Here's one with three subheads, and three columns of type, which he decides to read all at once:

The Textuality of Text. To what degree is the text aware of itself,[11] and how physical is the conceit itself? Does the project exist within its own space, or is it "completed" by the reader as a gesture

The Testicularity of Text. With the mere addition of a bicycle wheel in his hallway, the apartment suddenly takes on a hitherto unnoticed testicularity, creating a sort of visual musk. Hester McFaust

Meanings and Un-Meanings in the Textuality and Testicularity of Text. It should be noted that the incidence of prewar substance abuse on the East Coast had no bearing whatsoever on the

---

8. Whoops. My fault—I keep hitting this damn footnote button. Please continue.
9. Look, there's no point in these footnotes, so you might as well just ignore them.
10. Okay, now I'm just trying to annoy you.
11. A high degree, one would imagine. And yet, how aware are the footnotes? (See Nike's "Air on a Shoestring," Op. 9, Div. 6.)

of transgression between text and untext? (This question was put to the test at the end of the 1936 Berlin Olympics when French runner Monique Giroux suddenly noticed that clouds had the formation of shapes that seemed to have something to do with the alignment Hildegard notices the change immediately. Her earlier visit ended in a vague gender standoff, as Duncan Piedmont Carlsbad tried to assert his masculinity by means of cupping his genitals in an alarming Michael Jacksonian manner, which only served increased state of Artesian Avuncular Punctures (AAP),[12] which was then in a life-and-death struggle with their creditors at Amalgamated Pynchonian Bank (APB). Long before, the Baltimore Symphony Orchestra fired their finest violinists[13] of the era, which caused

When Blott awakes he realizes it's over three hundred pages later, and he's in a train in a tunnel, heading in some direction. He has no idea where. It doesn't matter. All he wants to do is read *Infinite Pest,* to see where it goes. What page is he on? Where is he?

---

12. Never mind.
13. Sorry—I keep doing this.

J. K. ROWLING

HARRY POTTER AND THE ROLLING STONE

The boys' uniforms department at Peter Jones was all out of Hogwarts ties, so Harry—who had singed his school tie in a fight with an irksome dragon—decided to try some other stores. He walked down Kings Road, past boutiques of silver suits and orange corduroy jackets, shoe stores that sold platform boots with goldfish in their heels, glitter pumps, and purple suede sandals. Harry smiled as he passed a pub called the Chelsea Potter—perhaps an ancestor had opened it centuries ago, when a group of early Potters had settled in the area.

He continued down the street, marvelling at the colourful and exciting shops, but not finding anything that he could even remotely hope to wear at school.

Then he came across a large modern building that seemed to be entirely covered in mirrors. A sign over the door identified it as the Chelsea Drug-store. Harry walked down the steps and through the shiny doors.

Inside, it didn't look like a drug-store at all. A maze of little stalls sold records and T-shirts, incense and small metal pipes that resembled plumbing supplies. Blaring out of the loudspeakers was a tune Harry recognized from the Top of the Pops, though he couldn't say he liked it much. He began flipping through a pile of magazines of pop stars and film actors as he vaguely noticed a small old shop-keeper beckoning him to come over. Harry ignored him.

"Psssst! Oy, you—come over here."

The man had long brown hair and huge lips and he seemed to jiggle and throb as he stood behind his stall, as if listening to some sort of secret tune in his head.

"Oy, you with the burnt tie—come 'ere . . ."

Finally Harry went over to the small man in a purple crushed-velvet suit and silver top hat.

"What do you want?"

"Why'd you set fire to your tie?"

"I didn't, I was in a fight with a—" Harry was about to explain how a couch he'd been sitting on had suddenly turned into a dragon, but he thought the better of it. "It just got burnt."

"I can help you with that. You don't want to go around looking like that. It gives a bad impression."

Harry looked at the clothes in the man's stall. There were shiny silk suits, top hats with glittered white stars and red stripes. There were scarves and white jumpsuits with corset strings and uniforms that looked—yes, Harry was sure of it—like they were used for playing American football. But there were no ties.

"What are all these things?"

"These are from my Rock 'n' Roll Circus," said the man. "Allow me to introduce myself. I am a man of wealth and taste. Name's Jack Flash. "

"How do you do, Jack Flash?"

"I do fairly well, actually."

"I'm Harry."

"Come out back, Harry. I'll see if I can find a tie for you."

Harry demurred, not so much out of dislike or distrust of Mr. Flash (after all, if he had ignored every unlikely offer, he wouldn't be where he was today). But he wasn't sure if he had time.

Sensing Harry's reluctance, Jack Flash quickly reached into the clothing pile and pulled out a couple of brightly coloured, wide psy-chedelic neckties, holding them up for Harry's inspection. "Whatcha think of these. Gear, right?"

Harry didn't want to seem unappreciative, but these ties were not right at all. "I'm not sure they're quite the correct colour," he said diplomatically.

"Very astute, Harry! That was just a test. We'd better check in the back. I think I've got something that might be a bit more . . . Hogwarts."

"But how did you know I go to Hogwarts?" inquired Harry.

"Ah! I can always tell a, um, *Hogwartian*," said Jack Flash cheerily. "Come with me."

Well, that did sound more hopeful, thought Harry. He followed Mr. Flash through a small orange door and into a dark, narrow corridor that was lit with odd overheard blue lights that made the white of Harry's shirt look like neon. He noticed that Jack Flash's silver hat glowed bright.

"Totally fab, eh? You should try it on acid."

Harry didn't say so, but he doubted the thrill could be enhanced by drinking acid.

The blue-light corridor led to another corridor, this one smaller and darker. Harry could hear the dull drone of drums in the distance, which echoed through the walls.

"Charlie's good tonight, ain't 'e?" said Jack Flash with a wicked smile.

Harry had no idea who Charlie was, but he was more concerned with his situation. "Where am I?" he said.

"Two thousand light-years from home," said Jack with a laugh, placing his hands on his hips and jutting out his bottom lip. Harry thought that next to Hagrid, this man had the biggest lips he'd ever seen.

"I should like to go home now, please."

Jack stuck out his tongue and wagged his finger. "You're very demanding, aren't you? Well you can't always get what you want. And if you try sometime, you just might find, you get what you need." And with that, he leapt up again and began trotting horselike on the spot. Harry thought this Jack Flash was very odd.

They now came out to a small courtyard with a swimming pool that had a car in it at the bottom.

"What's that?" asked Harry.

"It's a car in a swimming pool, ennit?"

"But what's it doing down there?"

"Brian drove it in. Didn't look where he was going, the silly git. Oops—one of the buttons on my trousers has fallen off. You wouldn't want my trousers to fall down, would you?"

Harry thought he didn't care about Mr. Flash's trousers one way or another.

"I should like to see the ties now," he said. But as he said this, he stepped on something that called out and moaned. "What was that?"

"Look out where you step!"

Harry looked down and saw he had stepped on a huge pile of putrefying muck. "Is that a compost heap?" asked Harry.

"No, that's Keith."

The pile blinked and Harry now saw the two eyes staring frostily at them. The muck parted and formed lips. A groan arose from the muck and then spoke. "What day is it?"

"It's Tuesday," said Flash.

"No, it's definitely Monday," said Harry.

The heap coughed and then closed its eyes. Harry assumed it had gone back to sleep.

"Is that what they teach you at Hogwarts? To step on everything?"

The drums had stopped now and the sudden silence seemed to depress Jack Flash.

"All right, take your clothes off, Harry."

"What?"

"You heard me. Off with them." And Harry now noticed the gun in Jack Flash's right hand.

He reached in his pocket for his wand, but it wasn't there. Then he remembered he'd left it in the pocket of his other jacket at school. Curses, he thought. He'd meant to buy another wand at Peter Jones, but had forgotten to do it.

"Hop to it, lad," said Mr. Flash impatiently.

Slowly, Harry began taking off his clothes, tossing the burnt tie aside. Jack Flash began undressing too. Quite soon they were both standing in their skivvies.

"Okay, hand them over."

Harry handed his jacket, shirt, and shorts to Jack Flash, who tried to squeeze into them.

"You can put mine on if you like."

Harry didn't much like the thought of wearing Jack Flash's clothes, but he figured it'd be better than standing around half naked in the cold. So he put them on. The silver jacket felt very large.

Jack was now squeezed into Harry's Hogwarts uniform, and Harry thought he looked very silly.

"Hullo! Hullo, I'm Harry Potter!" said Jack Flash in a ridiculously high voice.

"How do you know my name?"

"Oh everyone knows Harry Potter. You have the perfect demographic . . . *Everyone*." And he laughed, and repeated it: "Everyone." He reached into the pocket and a look of disappointment came across his face. "Where's the wand?"

"It's in my other jacket," said Harry.

Jack thought for a moment, his face squeezed into a scowl. "You can help me, little Harry."

"Help you? How?"

"I once had a merry band of minstrels, but the group fell apart. Charlie went back to his dogs and his wife—his first wife, if you please, whom he never even left in the first place. Bill retired to an old-age pensioners home in Blackpool after his son married his former mother-in-law. Brian drove into his swimming pool, Ronnie got sued by his own haircut, and Keith, as you saw, turned into a compost heap, gathering moss. And you know what they say about a Rolling Stone. Well, it's true. So it's just me now, running on the spot." Here he began running on the spot again.

"What do you want?"

"I want you to tell me the secret."

"What secret?"

"You know—the secret of synergy."

"Synergy doesn't work," said Harry.

"Oh yes, it does. You're flying proof. Let me have one."

"One what?"

And here Jack Flash felt so frustrated he almost sneezed. "A multimedia and cross-marketing deal with AOL–Time Warner!"

Harry turned crimson; talk of marketing always embarrassed him.

Jack was now dancing around the yard, pretending to be sitting on a broomstick. "Look at me! I'm Harry Potter playing Quidditch!" This was embarrassing too.

Harry thought about Jack Flash pretending to be younger, prancing about in front of people, and it formed an unseemly picture. How could he get this aging Pan with a creative comb-over a cross-marketing deal? Even Harry was getting a little long in the tooth for the kids these days; every six months they were on to a new action figure or boy band. He was thinking of retiring himself—after all, who wanted a nineteen-year-old boy wizard?

And yet . . . these silver clothes, these platform boots, stirred something within. He'd never had a band of minstrels, he'd never performed live in front of eighty thousand screaming fans. The hell with Hogwarts—he'd go on tour.

Just then a bald geezer with spectacles appeared from behind the shrubbery. "Oy, Jack. What's with the school threads?"

"Hullo, Charlie. Change of direction. I've decided to become Harry Potter."

"Does Keith know?"

And the compost heap rose up and shuddered. "What's the buzz?" said the heap.

The trio was now joined by a skeletal figure with a bird's nest on his head.

"Ronnie-Baby," said the heap. "The Flash is going frosty."

"Aren't we doing America next week?" said Ronnie.

Harry looked on in disbelief as the four men began squabbling. He subtly pointed an index figure at the bickering men and muttered under his breath:

> *"Brown sugar, tumbling dice,*
> *turn these minstrels into mice."*

There was a sudden thunder crack and then a burst of smoke filled the yard. When it cleared, the men had disappeared, replaced by four small mice clawing at one another and licking their fur.

Harry noticed also that his new clothes fit him better. He did a little jog on the spot. *This is gear,* he thought. He could place an advert in *Melody Maker* and his group could be rehearsing in a couple of weeks. Their emblem would be a burnt tie, and they'd go on Top of the Pops and tour the country. Then Europe and then America, followed by a crazed groupie and drug phase, and then clean up, and then a "Behind the Music" segment on VH1.

They'd need a name, of course. Harry gave it a good think. Harry and the Potheads? The Chelsea Potters? Harry and the Hogwarts? Hog Harry and the Warts?

No, he'd go by something more poetic, something that would easily roll off the tongues of children around the globe: *World Domination Pop Cultural Event!*

BRET EASTON
ELLIS

BOOKORAMA

"The club is called High School. It's actually a converted high school in the East Village."

"Uh-huh . . ."

"You have to dress like a teenager to get in."

"Everyone dresses like a teenager. But don't they already have this in London? A school night, when everyone has to wear their old school uniform?"

"Yes, but this is more than that. We have actors playing teachers. So you go to a class and you—well, you do what you'd do in high school."

"Goof off."

"Essentially. Talking. Beating up people in the hallways. Taking drugs in the bathroom. Feeling girls up in the utility closet. All the stuff you did in high school."

"What do you know about high school? Didn't you go to Dalton or something?"

"I grew up in L.A."

"Whatever. So this is your idea?"

"Yeah. Only it gets more interesting. A girl is found killed in the girls' room. At first they think she died of an overdose, but they later find out that she bled to death—giving birth to a baby. Who is also dead."

"She was giving birth in the toilet?"

"Yes. But she didn't realize she was pregnant."

"Okay . . . So we have an actress playing a dead girl and a doll playing the baby?"

"Yes. At first—but then it turns out that the actress playing the dead girl is actually dead—and the doll actually is a dead baby."

"That's pretty Gothic. Sort of *Scream* meets . . . Well, *Scream 2*. I'm not sure what casting agent would help you with that. Anyway, what's wrong with prep school? That way you can use all your usual tropes—wealth, status, fashion, and senseless murder. Plus the blurring of fact and fiction. And models."

The waiter came by—a model, who looked like a young Tom Cruise slumming as a waiter at the Mercer Kitchen. The author ordered a swordfish sushi and an Ottoman endive salad with Yugoslavian snails. The editor just had a Marienbad water. Richard Gere walked in with Christina Ricci. Gere wore a Hermès woven silk tie over a bias-cut shirt and an et Riviere leather jacket from Perry Ellis. Ricci had on an Ellen Tracy silver blouse with spaghetti straps and a gray skirt by Dolce & Gabbana. They stopped by Sting's table, where the pop star, wearing a Canali suit in Moroccan blue, was sitting with Keith Richards, in a fake leopard coat over a pair of red velvet trousers from Vestimenta, and Buddy Holly, wearing a black suit by Jil Sander and black glasses from LensCrafters. They waved to Robert De Niro (in a slate Armani double-breasted suit) and Dorothy Dandridge (wearing Victoria's Secret under a turquoise St. John sweater dress) across the room.

"Oh, I see," the editor said. "You have a dead icon motif going on."

"Sort of. But it's more than that."

"It is? How?"

"Um. It just is," the author said.

Suddenly the waiter lunged at them with a carving knife. John Holmes jumped up from his table, grabbed the knife from the waiter, and stabbed him in the neck. The blood splattered all over the editor, ruining his Calvin Klein suit. Holmes returned to his table, as if nothing had happened. None of the other diners had taken the slightest notice, even when other waiters came and dragged the dead waiter into the kitchen, leaving a smudged trail of blood on the floor behind them.

A new waiter appeared at the author and editor's table. He looked like a young Chris Isaak. "Can I get you any dessert?"

A shot rang out, and the waiter collapsed across their table. Blood soaked the white tablecloth, turning it red.

"Wow, this is quite an eventful meal," said the editor. He looked over and saw Andy Warhol put a Desert Eagle automatic back in his pocket. Warhol was wearing a black Brooks Brothers jacket, white shirt, Levi blue jeans, and white Converse sneakers. Did you see that?" said Andy. "Wasn't that just fabulous?"

The author smiled.

"I like the Warhol connection," said the editor, as two more waiters appeared and dragged off the shot waiter.

"Yes," said the author. "Warhol turns out to be a major character."

"A kind of art trope, reflecting the kitsch in the absurdity and moral ambiguity of the narrative," said the editor.

"Kitchen what?"

"Skip it. So who finances High School?"

"Oh, that's the great part. It's financed by a secret division of the CIA, which is training model/actresses as agents to kill foreign leaders."

"Didn't you do that in your last book?"

"Yes, but these are *vampires*," said the author enthusiastically.

"Oh."

Jayne Mansfield walked by their table and joined Monica Lewinsky and O.J. Simpson in a corner booth. Mansfield was wearing a jewel-encrusted bustier by Frederick's of Hollywood. Monica had on a brown plus-size Donna Karan dress and a pair of Prada thigh-high teal leather boots. O.J. wore a Tommy Hilfiger track suit and Manolo Blahnik shoes.

A Hollywood producer, who was responsible for covering up the deaths of several Vietnam immigrant children on the set of "Gook Island," stopped by Jayne Mansfield's table and told her how good she looked. "You can hardly see where the car sheered your head off."

"Thank you," she said with a giggle.

Suddenly an explosion could be heard from the street. A terrorist supergroup, comprising members of the Red Brigades, Symbionese Liberation Army, IRA, and Basque Separatists, charged through the doors of the restaurant-hotel. "Everyone down on the floor!" said a female terrorist in a khaki Versace Nehru jacket and white parachute pants by Luella Bartley.

The diners and waiters all hit the floor.

Under the table the editor looked for his Hugo Boss glasses, which had fallen off when he scrambled to the floor. He found them unbroken next to a shattered champagne flute, and slipped them on. "What's happening?" he asked the author.

"Military coup," said the author, who was also on his hands and knees under the table, grinning.

"What, in New York?"

"Yeah, it's part of a national terrorist takeover."

"That's ridiculous. None of the terrorist groups have anything in common. Half of them aren't even in existence anymore."

"It's surreal. General Custer isn't alive either, but if I'm not mistaken I have a feeling he's going to show up, right about . . . *now*."

The editor looked anxiously at the door, which soon opened, and General George Custer, his long blond hair tied in a ponytail, walked in. "Any Jews here?" he asked the crowd hiding under tables and chairs.

"What?" said the editor, surprised.

"Yes, he's anti-Semitic," said the author proudly. "See, it's a deconstruction of the terrorists myth, with a trope of anti-Semitics thrown in to confuse the equation."

"You don't know what you're talking about, do you?"

"All I know is this book is going to be a cause célèbre. A bête noire. Brad Pitt has already optioned it. Oliver Stone is killing to direct it. Literally. He shot a producer last week who was trying to get the film rights."

"But you haven't even written it yet."

"Oh it's written, all right. It's all up here." He tapped the side of his head. "Every word."

"So when are you going to write it? I want to see it."

"I don't intend to write it. That's *so* twentieth century. I'm going to improvise it at bookstore readings and then release it on DVD."

"Aren't you afraid of piracy?"

"My book is about piracy. My book *is* piracy. It represents the numbness of our amoral culture, and knocking it out of its complacency with terrorism."

"And models."

"Yes, and models."

The Mercer Hotel exploded and everyone was killed. A few moments later James Dean drove down Prince Street in his Hum-Vee and turned up Mercer Street—past a sign that said WRONG WAY.

ELMORE LEONARD

99 RULES FOR WRITING

1. Steal from the masters—they're probably dead so they can't sue you.
2. Only use two-word titles.
3. Quick Monkey.
4. Trouser Snake.
5. Never use a thesaurus.
6. Dinky Winky.
7. If you're gonna fake it, fake it *well*.
8. Gag reflex.
9. Brush your teeth after every meal.
10. Never write on the same side of the page twice.
11. Don't pretend you don't read your reviews.
12. Take the money and run.
13. No anthrax.
14. For "he said," never write, "he expostulated."
15. Alwayz uze spelchek.
16. Never stick a fork in a toaster.
17. If you don't know something, make it up.
18. Write in English.
19. Never begin a book with the word "Vociferously."
20. No footnotes.

21. No prologue.
22. No index.
23. No pop-ups.
24. No nineteenth-century woodcuts by Boz.
25. No expensive, limited editions with fake-fur covers.
26. No King of Pop.
27. No cats on the table.
28. Prepositions are your friends.
29. Adjectives are your enemy.
30. Posture, posture, posture.
31. Gut feelings.
32. Skid marks.
33. No baby talk.
34. No nookie between chapters.
35. Dunt tuse dia-lacht oonlass yer ken duit.
36. Never end a book with "and."
37. Or "but."
38. When typing, use as many fingers as possible.
39. When Shoreen brings a sawed-off shotgun to the airport, it's likely the metal detectors will find it.
40. Or maybe not.
41. Never accept a blurb from a federal agent.
42. Or Bret Easton Ellis.
43. No waking up to find it was all just a dream. Or was it . . . ?
44. Hire a lot of researchers with a quick-response team.
45. Pay them in doughnuts.
46. Floss.
47. If asked to sign a breast, never use a pencil.
48. Or an eraser.
49. Try to keep it under a pack a day.
50. Order small, tip big.
51. Use a zip disk.
52. No children called "Rumor" or "Scout."
53. No haute couture.
54. No garage wines.
55. No novelle cuisine.
56. Nothing macrobiotic.
57. No Yoga.

58. No Author's Commentary.
59. No director's cut.
60. No meetings.
61. Try to keep it under a pint a day.
62. But try the Long Island waffle cone.
63. Always check your cholesterol.
64. Honey, disconnect the phone.
65. Get back to where you once belonged.
66. Never bet the ace.
67. Beware the shill.
68. Look for the tell.
69. The lottery is for losers.
70. Don't forget to tip the super at Christmas.
71. Don't badmouth a cop who's stopped you for speeding.
72. If you've got it, show a little cleavage.
73. He who represents himself has a fool for a client.
74. Doctor Martens.
75. Eskimo Kiss.
76. Only a fool holds out for the top dollar.
77. If that's Quentin again, tell him I'm not home.
78. Don't take any wooden nickels.
79. Load the dice.
80. Load the bases.
81. Damn the torpedoes.
82. Cover your mouth when you cough.
83. Never ask Charlie Rose about his hair.
84. Recycle.
85. Soak.
86. Spit.
87. Never dive into a cold swimming pool right after you've eaten.
88. Risk factored.
89. Fools suffered gladly.
90. Never lose your cool.
91. Don't lose the remote.
92. Rush Limbaugh is a big, fat idiot.
93. Always keep your car keys in the same place.
94. Never put a Q-tip deep in your ear.

95. Keep the cigarette out of your author photo.
96. Always carry breath mints.
97. Wash behind your ears.
98. AOL sucks.
99. Clapton is God.